# AN INTRODUCTION TO
# CLINICAL SOCIAL WORK PRACTICE

# AN INTRODUCTION TO CLINICAL SOCIAL WORK PRACTICE

*By*

**JAMES E. LANTZ, M.S.W., PhD.**

*Assistant Professor*
*The Ohio State University*
*College of Social Work*
*and*
*Clinical Director*
*Village Counseling Associates*
*Columbus, Ohio*

**CHARLES C THOMAS • PUBLISHER**
*Springfield • Illinois • U.S.A.*

*Published and Distributed Throughout the World by*

CHARLES C THOMAS • PUBLISHER
2600 South First Street
Springfield, Illinois 62717

© *1987 by* CHARLES C THOMAS • PUBLISHER

ISBN 0-398-05334-0

Library of Congress Catalog Card Number: 87-1925

*Printed in the United States of America*
SC-R-3

**Library of Congress Cataloging-in-Publication Data**

Lantz, James E., 1943–
    An introduction to clinical social work practice.

    Bibliography: p.
    Includes index.
    1. Psychiatric social work—United States.    I. Title.
[DNLM: 1. Social Work. 2. Social Work, Psychiatric.
WM 30.5 L296i]
HV690.U6L36    1987        362.2'0925        87-1925
ISBN 0-398-05334-0

# INTRODUCTION

Clinical social work is alive and well. Professional social workers continue to provide direct service to thousands of individuals and families in a kaleidescope of treatment settings. In spite of the dire predictions made a decade ago, clinical social work remains relevant and important. We are the largest professional group which actively attempts to make sure that good mental health services are and remain available to the poor.

Clinical social work is a professional process rich in both problems and opportunities. We attempt to help client groups and populations who are often ignored and forgotten by mainstream America. Our task is difficult and frequently we receive minimal support from society at large. The clinical social worker is forced by the realities of his or her practice situation to remain creative while at the same time he or she draws upon the practice wisdom of our professional tradition.

It has been my attempt in writing this book to present a fairly clear introductory view of clinical social work as both a treatment philosophy and a treatment process. I have attempted to present an eclectic approach which remains systematic as it incorporates much of the old with some of the new. Analytic, interactional, reflective and action casework techniques are included in a structured and rational process. Self-awareness and respect for the client remain the most important treatment variables. I hope that this book is found useful to both the student and to the seasoned practitioner.

James E. Lantz, M.S.W., Ph.D.

# ACKNOWLEDGMENTS

Over the years it has been the author's pleasure to learn from many helpful and highly skilled significant others. These people include: Ernest Andrews, Joseph Fabry, Victor Frankl, Harold Mosak, Walt Pillow and Emanuel Schwartz. The author would like to thank Lawana Wimberly and Redonda Engel for excellent typing and consistent flexibility. The book is dedicated to Jan who is my love, my wife and my best friend.

# CONTENTS

# AN INTRODUCTION TO
# CLINICAL SOCIAL WORK PRACTICE

**Chapter One**

# SOCIAL FUNCTIONING

The purpose of clinical social work is to help individuals, families and other natural groups improve their social functioning. Social functioning refers to the interactions between and including the person and their social environment. This focus upon helping people improve their social functioning starts from the premise that a proper understanding of human behavior will include a balanced concern for the individual as a physical, spiritual, psychological and social entity (Turner, 1978).

Social functioning is a complicated process. It is not a static state of being, and it is constantly changing throughout the human life cycle (Lantz, 1978). No single factor can be identified as the primary and major influence upon the manifestation of social functioning. A complete and total understanding of human social functioning is at this time impossible to achieve. A partial understanding is only possible by utilizing a framework of multiple causation paired with a systems theory orientation of multiple feedback loops and reciprocal organic patterns (Satir, 1967) (Andrews, 1979) (Lantz, 1978A).

Social functioning is complicated yet very real. Dysfunctional social functioning patterns include, and are signaled by, intense human pain. Healthy patterns can include the height of human joy. Signals of social functioning problems can include anger, rage, depression, anxiety, physical illness, hallucinations, delusions, anomie, emptiness, suicidal thinking, drug addiction, alcoholism, human tissue damage, derealization experiences, starvation, and homicide.

Helping people to modify these patterns of social functioning is a difficult, rewarding and important human endeavor. Often it can become a literal matter of life and death. The activity of professional helping requires maturity, knowledge, self-awareness, responsibility and a high degree of social interest on the part of the professional social worker. Sensitivity, commitment, ethical behavior and controlled emotional involvement are additional terms used to describe the social worker's professional responsibility (Biestek, 1957).

There are many ways to describe, categorize, outline and/or conceptu-

3

alize the process of social functioning. Each way has its advantages and disadvantages. One method of outlining and organizing the components of social functioning is to categorize three primary social functioning components which are influencing factors, internal methods of defense or adaptation and interactional patterns of communication and/or problem solving behavior (Lantz, 1978). These three components and their relationship to each other are illustrated in figure number one. (See figure number one.)

The component of influencing factors refers to the multiple variables which can impact upon the process of social functioning. The component of internal methods of defense and/or adaptation refers to the perceptual, cognitive and executive aspects of human behavior (Dixon, 1979). The component of interactional communication and problem solving behavior refers to the emotional, verbal, physical and action aspects of human behavior (Lantz, 1980).

## Influencing Factors

Multiple causation is a term used to signify that social functioning is influenced by numerous variables. No single variable can ever accurately be described as the "one" factor influencing the manifestation of social functioning (Turner, 1978). Each influencing factor will always have a degree of significance in the origin and perpetuation of all human behavior. In different situations and problem forms each variable may take on a greater or lesser weight of influences, yet each variable will always retain a degree of significance.

An influencing factor can be considered as an internal or external influencing factor. Internal influencing factors include physical drives, physical health, developmental push and pace, social motivation, free will and central nervous system chemistry. External influencing factors include the person's social history, social situation, the cultural environment and the person's family environment.

## Physical Drives

The human being is a member of the animal kingdom. Like any other animal the human person has a desire to eat, drink, sleep, to engage in sexual activity and to protect its own existence. Other physical drives frequently identified by personality theorists include the aggressive

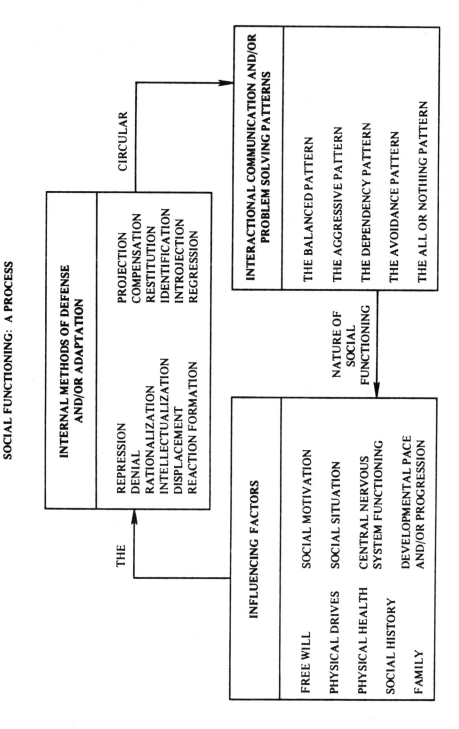

Figure 1

SOCIAL FUNCTIONING: A PROCESS

**INTERNAL METHODS OF DEFENSE AND/OR ADAPTATION**

| REPRESSION | PROJECTION |
| DENIAL | COMPENSATION |
| RATIONALIZATION | RESTITUTION |
| INTELLECTUALIZATION | IDENTIFICATION |
| DISPLACEMENT | INTROJECTION |
| REACTION FORMATION | REGRESSION |

THE

CIRCULAR

**INTERACTIONAL COMMUNICATION AND/OR PROBLEM SOLVING PATTERNS**

THE BALANCED PATTERN

THE AGGRESSIVE PATTERN

THE DEPENDENCY PATTERN

THE AVOIDANCE PATTERN

THE ALL OR NOTHING PATTERN

NATURE OF SOCIAL FUNCTIONING

**INFLUENCING FACTORS**

| FREE WILL | SOCIAL MOTIVATION |
| PHYSICAL DRIVES | SOCIAL SITUATION |
| PHYSICAL HEALTH | CENTRAL NERVOUS SYSTEM FUNCTIONING |
| SOCIAL HISTORY | |
| FAMILY | DEVELOPMENTAL PACE AND/OR PROGRESSION |

drive, the drive to learn, the drive for productivity, the drive towards intimacy, the drive towards identity and meaning and the drive towards finding sense and order in an often chaotic universe (Frankl, 1969) (Satir, 1967) (Horney, 1945) (Adler, 1927) (Rado, 1958). Some theorists (Freud, 1933) consider most of these drives to be a part of the sexual drive. Other theorists (Horney, 1950) (Satir, 1967) see such drives as a part of a larger human physical drive which can be called the life force or the drive towards growth and competence.

Over the years, personality theorists have struggled in an attempt to find out the degree to which human behavior is influenced by internal drives or by social forces. Often this struggle deteriorates into rigid black and white arguments which force attention exclusively upon either the internal drives or the external environmental factors. Neither extreme can be realistically considered accurate (Lantz, 1978).

In clinical social work the therapist recognizes that all people encounter both physical and social forces which effect their social functioning patterns. Physical and social forces are both considered important, yet it is recognized that both factors shape and direct each other in a reciprocal way. Neither type of influencing factor should ever be ignored (Turner, 1978).

## Physical Health

Many physical problems at first glance appear to be psychiatric problems. The loss of energy associated with blood circulation problems and cardiovascular disease can look like depression. Anxiety attacks are sometimes a signal which indicates the beginning stage of a heart attack. Anxiety can also be an indication of mitrovalve prolapse. Psychotic symptoms are sometimes created by a thyroid imbalance. Diabetic and epileptic seizures can resemble excited catatonia. Depression symptoms can be created by a lack of nutrition. Premenstrual syndrome can resemble manic-depressive illness. Hormonal imbalances are often signaled by depression. These and many other physical problems can easily be misdiagnosed and then referred to a clinical social worker for psychosocial therapy without medical involvement (Lantz, 1978B). On the other hand, prolonged stress reactive to environmental difficulties, psychological problems and maladaptive social functioning patterns can in fact create human tissue damage. Ulcers, muscular skeletal problems, high blood pressure, tacacardia, headaches, and dermatology difficulties are examples of physical health problems which are often considered reactive to problematic patterns of social living.

The clinical social worker should not serve as a medical diagnostician, or provide psychotherapy without medical consultation in clinical situations where physical illness or questionable symptoms exist. At the same time, it should be remembered that the clinical social worker does provide a diagnostic service and is a member of a diagnostic profession. In practical terms this means that when a clinical social worker receives a referral from a medical practitioner because the client's apparent medical problems are "just nerves," and the social worker believes that the client's physical difficulties can not be explained or understood in view of the client's social functioning patterns, the clinical social worker has every right to insist upon further medical evaluation and/or a second medical opinion. The clinical social worker also has a responsibility to refer the client for medical evaluation whenever the client presents a symptom or symptom cluster which could be reactive to, or creative of, a medical problem. It is this author's opinion that every clinical social worker should develop a workable, colleague relationship with a medical practitioner of internal medicine, psychiatry and neurology (Lantz, 1978B). The following clinical material illustrates the social worker's responsibility in this area.

### Mrs. Bower

Mrs. Bower was referred to a community mental health center by her family physician because "she is having a nervous breakdown and is a paranoid schizophrenic." The clinical social worker at the center agreed to evaluate Mrs. Bowers. Mrs. Bowers was brought to the emergency clinical interview by her husband. In the initial session the client stated that she was having visual hallucinations and "funny ideas." She stated that she was terrified that someone wanted to kill her. She stated that "I know this can't be true but it seems so real." The husband reported that Mrs. Bowers had never had any mental health problems, that there was not a history of mental illness in her biological family, and that Mrs. Bowers had always been in good health except for a few years when she was required to take thyroid medication. She had stopped taking thyroid medicine "a while back" when the family moved to a new town.

The clinical social worker did not believe that Mrs. Bowers was suffering from paranoid schizophrenia. Mrs. Bowers was 52 years old and had no prior history of this illness. Mrs. Bowers was trying to challenge her delusions. Mrs. Bowers was having visual hallucinations, rather than auditory hallucinations, and she had a history of thyroid problems in the past. The clinical social worker believed that Mrs. Bowers was having a thyroid psychosis and called the agency internal medicine consultant for evaluation help. The internist agreed with the social worker that thyroid psychosis was a "good possibility," and arranged to have Mrs. Bowers admitted to a medical floor rather than to the psychiatric unit of a general hospital. Tests were run and it was discovered that Mrs. Bowers did have a thyroid imbalance. Her apparent "symptoms of schizophrenia" disappeared when she was placed on thyroid medication.

## Central Nervous System Chemistry

It is now widely accepted that certain chemicals in the central nervous system are extremely important in the development of many forms of mental illness. These chemicals are called neurotransmitters and seem to be particularly important in the development of many affect disorders and schizophrenic disorders. In recent years, many authorities have concluded that neurotransmitter imbalances may have a significant role in the development of all of the psychiatric disturbances (Synder, 1980). Neurotransmitters are chemical molecules which help electrical impulses cross the synoptic gap from one nerve ending to the next nerve cell. In both major depression and schizophrenia it appears that neurotransmitter imbalances disrupt the normal brain processes of electrical impulses transfer from brain cell to brain cell. This in turn helps to create major distortions in human social functioning.

At the present time there are over thirty known chemical transmitters and authorities suggest that many more will be discovered in the following years. The importance of both the known, and yet to be discovered, neurotransmitters becomes increasingly clear when we remember that for many individuals adequate social functioning is not possible without the aid of psychiatric drugs. For example, schizophrenia is felt to be associated with an imbalance of a neurotransmitter called dopamine. Many of the antipsychotic drugs used to treat schizophrenia are considered helpful because they move to correct an imbalance of dopamine in the client's central nervous system (Torrey, 1983). The fact that thousands of schizophrenic people are now able to live away from the psychiatric hospital since the discovery of these medications is a true indication of the importance of biochemical factors in the development of this disease (Snyder, 1980) (Torrey, 1983).

The clinical social worker is not a medical practitioner and has no authority and sanction to prescribe medications. On the other hand, the clinical social worker should be able to determine when a client is showing symptoms which might respond favorably to medications. In such situations a referral to a psychiatrist for evaluation is appropriate and indicated. A second responsibility of the clinical social worker in this area is to recognize medication side effects. Many psychotropic medications do have uncomfortable and possibly damaging side effects. Often such side effects can be controlled by adding what is called an antiparkinson drug. Such drugs can help to control side effects of many of the psychotropic agents. The clinical social worker has a responsibility to "check in" with clients who are taking medication to see if side effects are a problem, and to then refer the client back to his or her psychiatrist for further evaluation. A number of excellent books are available for the non-medical psychotherapist who wants to learn more about this area of practice. Iron's (1978) book, *Psychotropic Drugs and Nursing Intervention,* is an excellent resource, as is Bockar's (1976) book, *A Primer for the Nonmedical Psychotherapist.*

## Developmental Pace and Progression

Developmental theorists such as Freud, Piaget, and Erikson agree that certain forms of learning tend to occur most effectively during certain stages of life. For example, Piaget feels that cognitive development follows a general set of stages beginning with sensorimotor learning (birth to two years), moving to preoperational learning (two years to seven years), followed by concrete operational learning (seven to twelve years), and ending with formal operational learning (twelve years and on). In Piaget's theory optimal learning opportunities for the different types of learning occur in different periods of time. Freud has postulated a time framework of psychosexual stages of development in which normal psychosexual conflicts emerge and are worked through. Each period of time has a corresponding conflict which emerges and is worked on by the developing person. Erikson has proposed eight psychosocial stages of life, each with an optimal time period for successful learning. Erikson's (1959) stages are called trust vs. mistrust, autonomy vs. shame and doubt, initiative vs. guilt, industry vs. inferiority, identity vs. role confusion, intimacy vs. isolation, generativity vs. stagnation, and integrity vs. dispair. Although all eight of Erikson's stages are important and can be worked on throughout a person's life, it is clear that each time of life has its central conflict and corresponding opportunity for specific conflict resolution.

The clinical social worker has a professional responsibility to be aware of the client's time of life and the particular learning opportunities and conflicts associated with each time of life. The client's progression through the life cycle can be blocked by both internal or environmental factors. The clinical social worker can become alert to such blockages only through knowledge of each life's stage's central cognitive, psychosocial and psychosexual issue (Lantz, 1978A).

## Social Motivation

Social motivation is a term which refers to the person's organized and consistent search for a personal sense of identity with both the self and with other people (Wheelis, 1958). Many personality theorists (Wheelis, 1958) (Horney, 1950) believe that this drive is internal and instinctual. Social motivation is a primary human drive which makes the feelings of intimacy and/or closeness with other people both extremely rewarding and extremely threatening (Wheelis, 1958). The drive is intense. If it cannot be fulfilled externally in a world of healthy human relationships, or if the client believes that it cannot be achieved with others, it will generally be fulfilled in an internal world of fantasy, or in a mechanical world of objects which are given symbolic social significance of the developing human being (Horney, 1945).

Social motivation can provide the worker and client a primary focus for treatment in clinical social work (Lantz, 1978A). Since the clinical social worker assumes that all people have a desire to find some method of achieving a significant relationship with both the self and others, the clinical social worker also believes that the client and therapist can generally find some common goal which can be worked upon during the treatment process. This sense of agreement which is based on the concept of social motivation does not mean that the social worker and client will always agree upon the who, what, why, when, where and how aspects of treatment. The concept of social motivation does not eliminate either conflict or resistance during treatment. It does, however, provide both the client and the social worker with an ever present opportunity to develop a treatment agreement based upon their common human desire for effective social living, meaning, a sense of purpose and the experience of a social identity.

### The Person's Family Situation

The person's family situation is considered to have a large influence weight by most clinical social workers. The human family provides the individual with his or her first and most basic sample of social interaction and social living experience. Communication rules, values and meanings, interactional skills, and human problem solving skills are demonstrated, modeled and experienced first in the individual's family of origin. Our first learnings about sex, intimacy, work, meaning, human closeness and conflict resolution occur in the family home or in a substitute family home (Lantz, 1978A) (Satir, 1967).

As we grow up and leave our original family home we begin to start a new social intimacy unit. We bring to the new intimacy unit a vast amount of previous social learning experiences. This learning then confronts and meshes with the past experiences of the new partner to create an original, unique and totally new family atmosphere. The new family or social unit takes on the psychological significance of our previous family and then begins to pass this significance on to the next generation (Lantz, 1978A) (Lantz, 1986C).

Social functioning cannot be effectively understood unless it is observed and evaluated within the family context of it's occurrence. A piece of human interaction which at first glance seems dysfunctional, or even crazy, can suddenly make tremendous sense when observed in it's context. For example, a medically normal baby who seldom cries may seem vocally lathargic until we learn that it's parents are deaf and cannot hear baby noises. The baby may have learned to "show" its feelings rather than to cry.

The individual's family is often the person's primary system of emotional support. Messages from the family group can have a great influence on the individual. Individual attempts to grow and change are frequently sabotaged by the family when the direction of change challenges family values and family rules (Andrews, 1974). Family social functioning patterns also can both reinforce or punish the individual when the individual decides or attempts to change. The family's feelings about an individual's request for treatment is often one of the most important variables that determine whether or not the treatment will be successful (Andrews, 1974).

## The Social, Environmental and Cultural Situation

The person's social situation refers to the social functioning and cultural tasks which confront each individual at the different stages of the person's life. Each new social functioning task that the individual must confront should be considered as both an opportunity for growth, and as a stressful situation. The stress of confronting the various social functioning tasks continues throughout a person's life. This ensures that each person always has a continuing opportunity to grow. Social functioning tasks that confront every human being include the task of work, the task of leisure, the task of intimacy, the task of socialization, the task of growing old, the task of learning to give to the next generation, the task of finding meaning in a chaotic world and the task of sexuality (Satir, 1967) (Adler, 1927) (Erikson, 1958).

The person's environmental situation refers to both the environmental opportunities and environmental difficulties encountered by the person in his or her passage through the life span. Much of our present functioning is done in a world which provides difficult hurdles to the unfolding of the human spirit. Poverty, war, economic instability, poor housing, inadequate health care systems, recession, inflation, hunger and sickness are all examples of environmental difficulties which can inhibit human growth. As Andrews (1979) has noted, there is always an association between an increase in psychiatric symptoms throughout the general population and the increased occurrence of stress triggered by the incidence of environmental, social and economic problems.

## The Person's Social History

Human beings utilize past social history experiences to structure present social functioning patterns on both a conscious and unconscious level of awareness (Horney, 1950) (Lantz, 1986C). Dysfunctional social functioning patterns from the past often represent the person's best adjustment in previous situations. They are maintained by the person during the present moment in time because their past use has provided the person with some benefit. Previously used dysfunctional patterns are hard to give up because they have provided the individual with a degree of comfort, they are familiar to the person, they are well practiced, they often operate on an unconscious level of awareness, and because the use of a new social functioning pattern is frequently accompanied by the occurrence of strong anxiety feelings (Lantz, 1978B).

It has been this author's observation that many therapists do not have a proper level of respect for resistance. Resistance to change is often seen as "bad" and viewed as simply something negative that needs to be overcome. Resistance can inhibit the occurrence of change but at the same time, it always has a protective function. Resistance can also be a message from the client to the clinical social worker telling the worker "You are on the right track in your attempts to help me." Resistance "resists" force, and is most often worked through if the client believes that the social worker has respect for the client's manifestation of resistance, and if the client believes that the social worker will not "take away" the client's defensive maneuvers without offering the client significant emotional support, as well as some alternative social functioning patterns that will work at least as well as the patterns which are to be discarded. Old patterns die hard for good reasons. Eliminating an old pattern without the addition of a new pattern results in a vulnerable client (Horney, 1950) (Lantz, 1980).

## Free Will

Free will is a term that refers to the human capacity to use choice in his or her responses to the environment or to the person's psychosocial situation (Frankl, 1969). Free will does not mean that the individual is totally free or that the individual has no limitations, boundaries or perimeters upon his or her behavior (Frankl, 1969). We are all limited by our physical capacities, our environmental situation, our culture and our time in history. Behavior is always partially determined by the contextual situation. Although every person must face specific limitations, it is accepted by the clinical social worker that each person does have the freedom to respond in a variety of different ways to each specific human or environmental limitation (Andrews, 1979). Such response freedom allows the person the opportunity to choose and also places the person into a position where the person is responsible for the choices that the person makes (Frankl, 1969) (Lantz, 1984A).

## Internal Methods of Defense and Adaptation

A person's internal methods of defense and adaptation include the perceptual, cognitive and executive aspects of social functioning (Dixon, 1979). These internal patterns and forms of human behavior have sometimes been labeled as ego operations (Dixon, 1979). The study of such ego operations is called ego psychology (Dixon, 1979).

Ego psychology is considered to be an outgrowth of psychoanalytic theory. It differs from classical psychoanalytic theory in that the classical theory places great emphasis on the instincts and the id, while ego psychology places more emphasis on the ego and the ego's relationship to the social environment (Dixon, 1979). Ego psychology is to a large part based upon the revolutionary work of Heinz Hartmann (Dixon, 1979).

Hartmann differed from Freud in that Hartmann believed that the ego has a genetic origin and that a part of the ego is always conflict free (Dixon, 1979). Freud (1933) believed that the ego evolved from the id and could not be considered as having a conflict free component. Hartmann believed that perception, intelligence, language and cognitive evaluation processes belong primarily to the ego (Dixon, 1979). These capacities allow the ego to perform its functions of survival and adaptation to the environment (Dixon, 1979). These capacities are the ego's primary autonomy apparatuses. They are considered to be independent of the id, and can mature in time as long as they are exposed to an average expectable environment (Dixon, 1979).

The innate ego apparatus provides opportunities for adaptation to the environment as long as the ego functions in an average expectable environment. When the ego is forced to deal with "massive" conflict, apparatuses of secondary autonomy come into play (Dixon, 1979). This means that the ego can use one or more of its apparatuses of primary function to change the function of an internal drive when it is in conflict with the superego, reality and/or the external environment (Dixon, 1979). This makes adaptation possible. It removes the drive from direct conflict with the environment and/or the superego. The ego also has the power to neutralize the aims and goals of the id, providing a second form of conflict resolution (Dixon, 1979).

Anna Freud and other ego psychologists have identified a number of specific ego defenses which can be utilized by the person to help the ego resolve conflict between the id and the superego and between the instincts and the environment (Dixon, 1979). Such defenses can be both helpful and harmful. The healthy ego is able to utilize a great number of defense mechanisms and is seldom forced to rely upon only one or two of these mechanisms. In this view, the functional use of many different defense mechanisms can be an indication of mental health. The rigid, inflexible use of only a few defense mechanisms is a sign of psychic trouble. A good rule of thumb for the clinical social worker to follow is to remember that the inflexible and rigid use of one or two defense mechanisms is a good signal of severe internal pain. The functional use of multiple defense mechanisms is often a good signal of ego strength (Lantz, 1978A).

## Repression

Repression is one of the earliest defense mechanisms observed by Freud. Ego psychologists consider this defense mechanism to be universal. It is utilized by everyone (Dixon, 1979). Repression is the process by which the ego pushes unacceptable drives, feelings and impulses into the unconscious. This prevents anxiety. For example, an employee may become very angry at his boss. If the degree of this anger is unacceptable to his superego or to the reality situation, the ego would push the feeling into the unconscious. This prevents the person from being aware of his anger, and prevents him from experiencing too much anxiety about the angry feelings. If the anger is too strong to be completely repressed, it may become manifest through passive-aggressive behavior and still remains out of the person's conscious awareness.

## Denial

Denial is similar to repression. In denial the person refuses, or fails to admit into conscious awareness, a feeling or event which actually exists (Dixon, 1979). Denial occurs in the preconscious level of awareness. Repression occurs in the unconscious level of awareness. Denial can be utilized to protect a person's sense of self-esteem or to protect the person from grief, anxiety or sadness. Denial often occurs in the form of disbelief when a person is faced with the impending death of a close relative or friend (Dixon, 1979).

## Rationalization

Rationalization is a process of finding or inventing excuses which minimize a person's sense of failure. It is often used to justify behavior that is unacceptable to the person's superego. It can be utilized in a situation where the person senses an upcoming failure, or in situations where the person believes that failure has already occurred (Dixon, 1979).

## Intellectualization

When using intellectualization the person turns unacceptable or painful feelings into abstract intellectual activities or discussions (Dixon, 1979). This defense may help the person become overly preoccupied with some abstract subject such as religion, philosophy or politics. This defense mechanism can "rob" the person of the opportunity for needed emotional expression (Dixon, 1979).

## Displacement

In displacement the person shifts feelings from the primary source to a different object because the person believes that directing them toward the real object or source is dangerous (Dixon, 1979). Displacement can occur with both positive and negative feelings. Scapegoating is a common form of displacement which occurs frequently in both organizations and families (Lantz, 1978A).

## Reaction Formation

In reaction formation the person engages in thoughts and feelings which are diametrically opposite of the person's real thoughts and feelings (Dixon, 1979). A common example of this defense mechanism occurs when a social worker who is angry at his or her client becomes overly protective, concerned and rigidly compulsive about the client's welfare.

## Projection

In projection the person believes that personal, painful or unacceptable feelings belong to someone else. A client who is angry at his therapist may project such feelings and then believe that the therapist is angry. This defense mechanism protects the person from painful feelings yet also cheats the person out of his or her opportunity to express and/or resolve such feelings (Dixon, 1979).

## Compensation

In compensation the person is somewhat aware of an unacceptable thought or feeling and then engages in exaggerated attempts to make up for the thought or feeling (Dixon, 1979). A person who feels inferior as an athlete, may "overtrain" or "overpractice" in an attempt to become a "distinguished" athlete or "superstar."

## Restitution

In restitution the person attempts to provide amends to another person or group for personally unacceptable feelings, thoughts or behavior. In this way the person can relieve guilt feelings about his or her perceived transgressions (Dixon, 1979). Restitution can be a useful defense, yet it is problematic in that it continues to occur as long as the person continues to feel guilty. At times it can turn into a compulsive mechanism with little personal or social value.

## Identification

Identification is a process in which the person takes on the characteristics of a loved and/or admired significant other. The person then makes these characteristics into an integral part of the self (Dixon, 1979). Identification helps to dissapate feelings of low self-esteem. Identification can be positive or negative. It is a universal human process. Clinical practitioners who are aware of this defense mechanism often take "extra care" to provide positive modeling experiences for there clients (Lantz, 1984A).

## Introjection

Introjection is a special form of identification in which the person internalizes the feelings of others and then experiences these feelings as a part of the real self (Dixon, 1979). Introjection is frequently the process at work when a child attempts suicide following the suicide of a parent.

## Regression

In regression the person goes back to the manifestations of feelings and behaviors utilized in an earlier stage of the person's psychosocial development. Regression is the process at work in the situation of a toilet trained child who has frequent toilet "accidents" following forced separation from a parent or the birth of a new baby sister or brother. Regression can be a helpful defense mechanism. It is often utilized by social workers at the end of a stressful week when they go the weekly "thank God it's Friday" ceremony and act "crazy." This is sometimes called regression in the service of the ego (Dixon, 1979).

## Interactional Communication and Problem Solving Patterns

Human interaction is complex. It encompasses a person's thinking, feeling, and behavior as well as such similar activities performed by the person's set of significant others. Human interaction is a continuous and reciprocal process. It proceeds as long as human life exists. Even silence is a special form of human interaction.

Human interaction can never be completely understood. It is exquisitely complicated. It occurs on many different levels, in many different forms, and in many different varieties. It is common place, yet at the same time it is always unique, and in some way always original. Since human interaction can never be completely understood, it is fair to state that no model that attempts to clarify human interaction will ever be totally useful or completely valid. In spite of these limitations, model development attempts can still be valuable. Such models can help us learn to observe human interaction in a more accurate and systematic fashion. One model that can be useful in our efforts to observe and understand human interaction is to identify patterns of movement within human interaction and human problem solving. Karen Horney (1945) (1950) has provided one such model.

## Movement Patterns in Human Interaction and Problem Solving

Horney (1945) (1950) identifies three forms of movement in human interaction. The three forms are moving towards other people, moving away from other people, and moving against other people. It is important to note that all three patterns of movement in human interaction can have both positive and negative benefits for the interacting human being. Moving towards other people can result in intimacy and/or dysfunctional forms of dependency. Moving against other people can result in assertive behavior and/or dysfunctional aggression. Moving away from other people can result in self-reliance and/or dysfunctional isolation. Horney (1945) makes the point that these three patterns should not be considered as good or bad, as all three patterns can result in both functional and dysfunctional human and social consequences. Horney (1945) also points out that healthy human interaction includes a flexible and balanced use of all three patterns. A flexible and balanced use of all three interactional movement patterns provides the person with flexible social living skills (Lantz, 1978A) (Lantz and Treece, 1982). Such flexibility allows the person to adapt to his or her environment as the environment changes. This flexibility also improves the person's ability to change the environment. The development of rigid and inflexible pattern of human interaction inhibits the person's capacity to problem solve in a modern world of rapid and continuous change (Horney, 19545) (Lantz and Treece, 1982).

Horney's description of interactional movement patterns can be expanded to develop a human interactional typology that includes five categories or forms of human social interaction. These categories are the balanced form, the attaching form, the avoiding form, the dependency form, and the all or nothing interactional form.

## The Balanced Social Functioning Movement Pattern

In the balanced pattern the person develops an interactional problem solving style that includes a balanced and flexible use of moving towards other people, moving against other people, and moving away from other people. The individual is able to be intimate with others and also to be appropriately dependent upon others. The individual is also able to be aggressive and/or assertive with other people in a way that does not infringe upon the rights of other people. The individual is able to avoid other people when this is appropriate, and does not fear the experience of spending time alone.

The balanced interactional movement and problem solving pattern includes a balanced affect or feeling experience. In the balanced feeling experience the individual is able to experience the feelings of anger, anxiety and depression. At the same time the individual seldom develops an extreme, rigid, and/or continuous feeling experience of just anger, just anxiety, or just depression. In this pattern the individual can use anger or aggression to facilitate moving against other people when this pattern is appropriate. The individual can use the affective experience of anxiety to help in moving away from other people and problems when this pattern is appropriate, and the individual can use the affective experience of depression or dependency feelings to help in moving towards other people when this pattern is appropriate. This connection between the different movement patterns and the different feeling states is based upon the "action facilitation theory of emotions" originally proposed by Rado (1958A). It should also be noted that the balanced feeling or affect experience is generally found in connection with both the balanced interactional movement pattern and with the human experience of overall happiness (Rado, 1958A). Another important point to note is that within the balanced movement pattern and the balanced feeling experience pattern, the individual does not generally manifest the extreme form of any single emotional or behavioral pattern (Rado, 1958A). For example, the extreme form of moving against other people is murder and murderous rage. This extreme form of feeling and social movement is not included in the balanced interactional and feeling experience pattern. The balanced communication and problem solving pattern is generally associated and compatible with the person's use of multiple internal defense mechanisms. The person is flexible in both the use of internal and interactional methods of adaptation (Lantz, 1978A).

This balanced pattern of interactional movement is the most healthy form of human communication (Horney, 1945) (Lantz and Treece, 1982). In this pattern the person maintains an appropriate degree of both stability and flexibility which is extremely important in effective social living. The development of a balanced interactional and social functioning pattern is a primary treatment goal in clinical social work (Lantz, 1980).

## The Attacking Pattern

In the attacking interactional movement pattern the individual has developed a style of attacking other people whenever the individual experiences any insecurity, unhappiness or social functioning problem. In this pattern the individual has overdeveloped his or her use of aggression. The primary feelings that are experienced by the individual in this movement pattern are anger and rage. The individual has also developed a symbolization pattern of blaming others for all problems and in this pattern the individual believes that it is fair to "get the other person first, before they get me." The extreme form of this pattern is actual murder accompanied by murderous rage. In this pattern the individual has underdeveloped his or her use of the moving towards other people pattern and also has underdeveloped the use of the moving away from other people pattern. As a result the individual who uses the attacking interactional pattern seldom experiences a great deal of anxiety or depression. At the first experience of either anxiety to depression the individual will generally switch to the feeling state of rage or anger and will scan his or her environment for someone to attack and blame. Projection and rationalization are common defense mechanisms associated with this social functioning pattern.

In the attacking pattern the individual has generally developed a suspicious picture of the world. The person believes that other people cannot be trusted. The individual also frequently develops a grandiose sense of his or her own importance. Such a person generally believes that they are the center of the universe and that other people are less important. This grandiose sense of self most often hides a very poor self-concept on a deeper and unconscious level of awareness. An important treatment goal when working with the attacking pattern client is to help expand the individual's use of avoidance and dependency patterns while helping the individual decrease his or her primary reliance upon the attacking pattern.

## The Avoiding Pattern

In the avoiding pattern the interacting human has developed a style of moving away from other people as a primary way of solving problems. In this pattern the individual has overdeveloped his or her use of avoidance and isolation. The primary feeling state experienced by the individual with an avoiding pattern is anxiety. In this pattern the individual frequently develops symbolization processes which include the belief that the world is "dangerous" and that other people will "use me." The person also is frightened that other people will "hurt me." The individual frequently has developed a poor self-concept. In addition, the individual also sets minimal self-ideal expectations as his or her social functioning goals. The general idea in the avoiding pattern is to avoid stress, problems, people, and expectations. The person believes that "I cannot compete."

In the avoiding pattern the individual views the self as weak and the environment as dangerous. Such symbolizations trigger a chronic and ongoing state of anxiety. This state of anxiety is magnified whenever the person begins to encounter stressful events, problems, people who desire closeness, people who exhibit anger or people who show demands. As this anxiety process is amplified there is an immediate increase in the person's use of avoidance. This use of avoidance increases until the stressful event "goes away" or the stressful people "give up" and retreat. At this point the anxiety decreases to a more comfortable yet ongoing and chronic level. A primary treatment goal in this pattern is to help the client decrease his or her primary use of avoidance and to help the client increase his or her ability to be both assertive and to develop an increased sense of closeness with other human beings.

## The Dependency Pattern

In the dependency pattern the interacting human has developed a social functioning style of moving towards other people as a primary way of solving social functioning problems. The individual has overdeveloped his or her use of relying upon other people to solve personal problems. The individual becomes extremely skilled at getting other people to provide support and to accomplish tasks. The dependency pattern individual has also been described as a "leaner" (Mosak, 1979).

In many instances it is found that the person who uses the dependency or leaning pattern, has suffered significant loss at an earlier stage of psychosocial development. Such individuals suffer from chronic states of depression which are amplified whenever the individual faces social or internal stress. Stress triggers an amplification of the person's depression which in turn triggers an increase in the person's use of the dependency or "leaning" pattern. Symbolization patterns frequently encountered when working with the individual who uses the dependency pattern include a low self-concept, a self view of "I am weak," and the idea that others are always "stronger and better." A primary treatment goal is to encourage such clients to manifest self-reliance and assertive patterns of human behavior. Such individuals will not tolerate treatment unless the professional helper meets some of their dependency needs.

### The All or Nothing Pattern

In the all or nothing pattern the interacting human being has learned to use at least two, and frequently three, movement patterns in their extreme form. Such individuals can get very angry and then use this anger or rage to facilitate an extreme form of movement against other people. Such individuals can also develop severe feelings of depression or anxiety and can then use such feelings to facilitate an extreme form of movement against other people. Such individuals can also develop severe feelings of depression or anxiety and can then use such feelings to facilitate an extreme form of movement towards or away from other people. The all or nothing client is unable to use moderate feelings or moderate interactional movement patterns. The middle group of feelings and movement is unfamiliar territory. Such individuals develop symbolization patterns that include "black and white" and "all or nothing" forms of thinking. Splitting is a defense mechanism frequently utilized by the person who uses the all or nothing pattern (Masterson, 1976) (Rowe, 1980).

The all or nothing client has an exceptionally difficult life. Such individuals experience intense feeling shifts and frequent crisis situations during their daily existence. They can be described as having a chronic but crisis form of social living. These individuals experience severe "feeling storms." They often feel overwhelmed by their emotions and believe that they have little control over such feelings. Such individuals have often suffered extreme forms of abuse, neglect and abandonment in their earlier developmental years (Rowe, 1980) (Masterson, 1976).

Symbolization patterns encountered when working with the "all or nothing" client include ideas such as "I am weak," "I am evil," "people are dangerous," "the world is evil," "I must be prepared to strike first," "I must hide," and "I need you to survive." Symbolizations are usually extreme and seem to match up with the client's exaggerated feeling and interactional movement patterns. Such individuals are often labeled in psychiatric settings as borderline personality disorder clients (Rowe, 1980) (Lantz and Thorward, 1985).

The primary treatment goal when working with the "all or nothing" client is to help the client develop a moderate or middle of the road approach to social living. Treatment with this type of client is generally long, stormy, difficult, and at times extremely rewarding. The beginning therapist does not generally do well with this kind of client and should not work with this type of client unless he or she is closely supervised by an experienced worker.

### The Circular Nature of Social Functioning

Social functioning is a circular process. Influencing factors mold the manifestation of defense mechanisms. Defense mechanisms shape the interactional problem solving patterns, and these patterns then effect and mold the influencing factors. The circle goes around and around throughout the life cycle. The circle of social functioning can be a circle of growth, or it can become a circle of despair. Happiness grows happiness. Poverty grows poverty. Depression grows depression. Identity grows identity.

It is the task of the clinical social worker to help the client interrupt, challenge, change and redirect the vicious circle of personal and social despair. Such a task is difficult and such a task is also extremely rewarding when it is achieved.

Chapter Two

# CURATIVE FACTORS
# AND TREATMENT TECHNIQUES

A curative factor can be defined as a treatment process which directly stimulates client change (Yalom, 1970). A curative factor is different than a treatment technique or a treatment modality in that the technique or modality does not directly stimulate the occurrence of change but instead sets up the type of treatment atmosphere in which the actual curative factor can emerge (Frank, 1961). The purpose of this chapter is to identify and describe a number of curative factors which occur in social work practice and to also describe a variety of treatment techniques which can stimulate the emergence of the various curative factors. Treatment modalities will be discussed in Chapter three.

## Curative Factors

After reviewing a number of curative factor typologies, (Yalom, 1970) (Andrews, 1972) (Hollis, 1972) (Frank, 1961) (Gedo, 1979), four curative factors have been identified which are particularly relevant to the process of clinical social work. These curative factors are called prestige suggestion, support, experiential validation and insight (Lantz, 1986A).

## Treatment Motivation and The Curative Factors

A constant observation reported by many supervisors, researchers and experienced practitioners is that the beginning direct service worker will frequently fail to engage the client in the treatment process by not individualizing treatment to the client's emotional needs (Lantz, 1986A). Such a failure is also considered to be a primary indication of dysfunctional countertransference when manifested by experienced workers (Rado, 1958B). Engagement failures have been observed at both the beginning of treatment and also during all stages of the social work process. They have been explained as resulting from countertransference feelings, inexperience, improper or inaccurate assessment or the overzealous adherance to any single philosophy of treatment. Rado (1958B) points out that engagement failures can also result from an improper understanding of the client's motivation for treatment and that psychoanalytic theory may well have contributed to such misunderstandings by failing to point out, or stress, the adaptational components of the client's motivation and/or transference manifestations. Rado (1958B) has developed a motivational framework which can be utilized and expanded by the direct service worker to help the worker more effectively individualize treatment. In Biestek's (1957) terms, such a framework can help us "start where the client is at." Such a framework can help us determine the client's developmental fixation or regression level, a curative factor which will be initially most supportive to the client and those treatment techniques which have the greatest potential to stimulate the emergence of a supportive curative factor. The four types of treatment motivation described by Rado (1958B) are magical craving, parental invocation, cooperative striving and realistic self reliance. (See figure number two.)

Rado's motivational framework is designed to categorize the client's emotional motivation for treatment. As in every other categorization tool the categories listed are not perfect, and there will never be a client who perfectly fits into any of the categories at all times. In this framework every client who requests treatment, or who accepts even a forced referral, has some form of treatment motivation. The form of the initial motivation may not fit with either the agency's or the worker's ideas about what is a "good" form of motivation. Even so, the client's presence at the agency, or with the worker, does indicate a form of treatment motivation (Lantz, 1986A).

The client's form of treatment motivation usually includes both transference and adaptational components. For example, a client who is motivated to simply get the worker to "take care of me" is usually manifesting a form of transference. At the same time this motivational approach is often adaptive. It may represent the client's "best attempt" or "best form" of social functioning. Asking the client to change his or her treatment motivation prior to the start of the helping process is similar to asking the client to no longer need treatment before treatment has started (Lantz, 1986A).

If the worker can understand and accept the adaptational qualities of the client's motivation, the worker can then join with the client in at least a beginning treatment alliance. Resistance is minimized and the opportunity to help the client develop a more functional form of treatment

Figure 2

CURATIVE FACTORS AND CLIENT EMOTIONAL MOTIVATION FOR TREATMENT

| EMOTIONAL MOTIVATION FOR TREATMENT | CORRESPONDING DEVELOPMENTAL LEVEL | MOST SUPPORTIVE CURATIVE FACTOR |
|---|---|---|
| MAGICAL CRAVING | INFANT | PRESTIGE SUGGESTION |
| PARENTAL INVOCATION | CHILD | SUPPORT |
| COOPERATIVE STRIVING | ADOLESCENT | EXPERIENTIAL VALIDATION |
| REALISTIC SELF-RELIANCE | ADULT | INSIGHT (DEVELOPMENTAL AND/OR EXISTENTIAL) |

motivation will not be lost to a premature termination. In addition, such an approach allows service opportunities to remain open to those clients who really are unable to change their form of treatment motivation due to factors beyond their control (Lantz, 1986A).

### Prestige Suggestion and Magical Craving

The first form of treatment motivation described by Rado (1958) is magical craving. In this motivational form the client expects the worker to perform a miracle. In many instances the client will project magic powers on to the worker and will then feel better, not because the worker has done anything to help, but because the client believes that the worker can, and has, performed magic.

The magical craving client does not understand cause and effect thinking, at least on an emotional level. Such clients often have a thought disorder. They engage in magical thinking, exhibit ideas of reference, and frequently experience both delusions and hallucinations. Such clients are often diagnosed as suffering with schizophrenia, borderline personality disorder, or with a schizoid personality disorder. They are either fixated or have regressed to the infant stage of psychosocial development. They experience massive levels of anxiety in their daily life. Rado (1958B) makes the point that under stressful conditions every human being can regress to this motivational level.

The curative factor which is initially most supportive to the magical craving client is prestige suggestion. In this curative factor the worker does not need to try to perform, or to say, that he or she can perform magic. Instead the worker allows the client's magical expectations of success to trigger or facilitate an improvement by suggesting a few things the client can do that will "somehow" help. The curative factor of prestige suggestion can be facilitated by the use of indirect suggestion, charismatic permission, and by symbolic structure and ritual. The following case material illustrates the curative factor of prestige suggestion in work with a magical craving client.

### Sally

Sally is a 28 year old client with the clinical diagnosis of borderline personality disorder. She experiences massive levels of anxiety in reaction to any form of separation. She has extremely strong anxiety attacks when her ongoing worker goes on vacation or is sick. At this point in her treatment she has great difficulty tolerating emotional separation and/or symbolic separation. In the past she has used wrist slashing to handle her anxiety about separations. Prior to her worker's last vacation he gave Sally a small figurine to "hold on to until I get back." Sally was instructed to "look at the figurine and hold it if you start having anxiety attacks while I am on vacation." When the worker returned from his two week vacation Sally informed him that the figurine was "magic" and that if she simply looked at the figurine she felt more comfortable. Sally did not slash her wrists while the worker was gone. Some authorities (Frank, 1961) would say that the worker gave Sally a transitional object. The use of this symbolic ritual or transitional object was effective because of Sally's magical craving.

## Support and Parental Invocation

Parental invocation is a little higher up on the motivational ladder. Parental invocation is similar to the child developmental stage in which the child strongly relies on his parents. This is still a primative adaptational level in that the client needs to rely upon a stronger, significant other. In the parental invocation motivational state the client will attempt to get the worker to do everything for the client. The client expects the problem to be solved, not by magic, but through the worker's efforts rather than the client's efforts (Lantz, 1986A) (Rado, 1958B).

The parental invocation client understands cause and effect thinking but does not believe that he or she has the power or skill to influence a personal psychosocial situation. Strength and solution must come from the worker. Such clients are frequently psychotically depressed. They are often diagnosed as suffering with a major or endogenous depression. Again, Rado (1958B) makes the point that under the proper level of stress every person can regress to this motivational level.

The curative factor which is initially most supportive to the parental invocation client is support. In this curative factor the worker does not reject his or her giving role. Initially the client is not challenged to take on more personal responsibility. The client's need for support is met through the use of worker empathy, ventilation acceptance, listening, encouragement, and environmental manipulation. The following case material illustrates the curative factor of support used with a parental invocation client.

## Bill

Bill requested social work services after the death of his father and after his wife "ran off with another man." Bill reported that he worked full-time, that he had two kids to take care of, and that he felt very depressed. He stated that he was overwhelmed and needed help. He reported suicidal thinking, crying spells and confused thinking. The worker arranged for Bill to see a psychiatrist who placed Bill on an antidepressant medication. The worker also called a child welfare agency to help Bill get homemaker and child care services. Initially Bill was given three appointment times per week with the worker so that Bill could express some feelings and talk out his frustrations. The worker's attitude was supportive. Concrete environmental services were also arranged. Bill made excellent progress. Within two months the symptoms of depression were gone and Bill stated that he felt like "I can handle the stress." Bill told his worker that "when I was really down and out you helped by giving me support." He also stated that it helped when the worker "took over" and made some arrangements that "I couldn't do myself." Both emotional support and concrete environmental services were indicated because Bill was overwhelmed and needed "someone else to do something." Under stress Bill had regressed to the parental invocation level of motivation.

## Experiential Validation and Cooperative Striving

Cooperative striving is the next stage in the motivation hierarchy (Rado, 1958B). In this motivational level, the client does not want the worker to do anything, but wants the worker to "tell me what to do." The client wants direction, advice, and suggestions. The client feels strong enough to do the work but does not feel adequate to figure out what work to do. The cooperative striving stage is reminiscent of adolescence. In this stage, the client wants autonomy of action but is not comfortable with either goal setting or with identifying effective solution techniques (Lantz, 1986A).

Many of our social worker clients come into treatment with this form of treatment motivation. They do not want the worker to run their life, but they do expect the worker to provide adequate direction and guidance. Such clients are usually diagnosed as crisis clients, adjustment disorder clients, or as neurotic. Clients who request marital or family therapy often manifest this form of treatment motivation (Lantz, 1986A).

The curative factor which is initially most supportive to the cooperative striving client is experiential validation. Experiential validation can be defined as a process of interactional or problem solving experimentation in which the client emotionally learns which adaptive solutions work best and feel best (Andrews, 1972). Treatment techniques which can be utilized to facilitate this curative factor include confrontation, pattern clarification, social skill training, cognitive restructuring, and behavior modification (Lantz, 1986A). The following case material illustrates the curative factor of experiential validation with a cooperative striving client system.

### Joan and Sam

Mr. and Mrs. Smith requested marital therapy because "we want to improve our communication." Joan stated that she was shy and that she got very anxious when she talked about problems or feelings. Sam stated that he never had been comfortable with conflict and that he tended to avoid it whenever possible. Both Sam and Joan wanted the worker to "give them suggestions" about how to talk with each other about feelings, conflicts, and problems. The worker gave Sam and Joan the following "advice." They were told that the worker felt it best if they came to marital therapy once a week and used the marital sessions as a practice laboratory in which to experiment and find ways to talk about feelings with each other. The worker advised the couple that he would be making lots of communication suggestions but that it would be up to them to "try it out in lab" and to "see how it feels." The couple made good use of marital therapy and discontinued treatment after five months of "practice."

### Insight and Realistic Self-Reliance

The client who demonstrates the motivation of realistic self-reliance is not interested in magic, concrete help, or worker advice. This type of client wants to "figure it out for myself." Such clients want to use treatment as a method of discovering how to make full use of their own inner potential (Rado, 1958B). Such clients are usually described in the literature as growth-oriented clients. Their motivational level corresponds with adulthood. Such clients are interested in insight (Lantz, 1986A)

(Redo, 1969). They frequently want an analytic or existential approach to treatment. Many social work practitioners request this form of personal treatment and the waiting list at most analytic institutes is filled with individuals who desire such an experience.

The curative factor which is initially most supportive for the realistic self-reliance client is insight. Insight can be developmental or it can be existential. Treatment techniques which stimulate such curative factors are genetic and transference interpretations, encounter experiences during the treatment relationship, and the socratic search for meaning (Lantz, 1986C). The following clinical material illustrates the curative factor of insight when working with the realistic self-reliance client.

### Amy

Amy is a 29 year-old single female who graduated with a master's degree in social work when she was 26. She has been working at a community mental health center for the past two years. She states that she does good work but has noticed that certain kinds of clients "make me nervous." She states that she is uncomfortable with her own anger and that she gets nervous around female clients who "have the same difficulty." Amy wants to increase her self-awareness so that she does not experience so much "countertransference." Amy was seen a few times in individual treatment and was then referred into an interactional awareness group. She has been able to use the group experience to learn more about her dependency feelings, her anger, and her interpersonal relationships with both men and women. Amy's self-reliant motivation for treatment, and her focus upon insight, makes her an excellent candidate for this nondirective, process group.

### Treatment Motivation, Support and Confrontation

Clinical social work treatment almost always provides the client with the opportunity to experience all four of the major curative factors. Rado's (1958B) emotional motivation for treatment framework can help the clinical social worker determine which curative factor will initially be most supportive to the client. The framework can also help the practitioner identify which curative factor will maximize confrontation and client discomfort when this is indicated. When the practitioner uses treatment techniques which stimulate the development of a curative factor which is compatible with the client's treatment motivation, then support is maximized. When the worker uses treatment techniques which stimulate a curative factor which opposes the client's treatment motivation, then confrontation is maximized. Rado's (1958B) framework can give the practitioner a useful tool which will help the worker become more sensitive to the balance of supportive and confrontation elements as they occur throughout the treatment process (Lantz, 1986B).

## Treatment Techniques

A treatment technique is a tool used by the therapist to stimulate the occurrence or emergence of a curative factor (Yalom, 1970). Treatment techniques can be used by the therapist in two distinct ways. The treatment technique can sometimes be used inappropriately as a gimmick to trick the client into change. The use of the treatment technique as a gimmick often occurs after the therapist has recently learned a new technique and attempts to use the client to practice the technique, in spite of the fact that the technique might not be appropriate for the client. The therapist can also use a treatment technique to "beat the client into change." In such an instance the therapist is using the technique in an indirect way for the expression of the therapist's hostility (Andrews, 1979).

Every treatment technique can be used as a gimmick. This usage of a treatment technique generally occurs whenever the therapist sees the client as an object to be manipulated rather than as a human being in need of help (Yalom, 1980). The "gimmicky" use of any treatment technique is reductionistic and can easily damage the client-therapist relationship (Andrews, 1979). Any manifestation of resistance by the client in response to reductionistic activities on the part of the therapist should be considered as a client strength. A second way to use a treatment technique is to use it humanistically. The humanistic use of a treatment technique occurs when the technique to be used is compatible with both the client's need and with the therapist's personality (Andrews, 1979) (Lantz and Thorward, 1985).

Treatment techniques can also be viewed as falling into two major categories which are labeled as being empathic category techniques and action category techniques. An empathic form of treatment technique helps the therapist understand the client, helps the client feel that he or she is being understood, and helps to promote client insight, self-awareness and self-esteem. Empathic techniques help the client change internal defense mechanisms. An action type of treatment technique helps the client develop increase flexibility and balance within the movement component of social functioning.

Hundreds of different kinds of treatment techniques are available for the therapist to use in his or her attempts to help the client change (Frank, 1961). A complete listing of every technique which could be used by the clinical social worker is impossible, and most probably inappropriate. The following treatment technique descriptions are presented in order to give the reader a "taste" of the rich variety of techniques which can be used by the clinical social worker in order to help the client increase flexibility and balance in the client's social functioning.

## Activity Therapy Techniques

Activity therapy techniques are primarily designed to increase client learning through the use of action and or movement (Fidler and Fidler, 1978). Activity therapy techniques can stimulate insight and can also be used to help the client practice a new style of social interaction (White, 1971). Activity therapy techniques are most often used as an action technique but at times can be used as an empathic technique. The following case illustrates the use of an activity called "log sawing" to help an aggressive pattern client practice a new form of social interaction.

Mr. Shilmer requested admission to a psychiatric hospital because he was experiencing feelings of rage and was having temper outbursts. Mr. Shilmer evidenced no signs of medical or neurological difficulties. His primary therapist considered him to be a person who had developed unrealistic feelings of entitlement which he handled by using a rigid and inflexible pattern of moving against other people in his social and problem solving operations. Mr. Shilmer was assigned to daily log sawing as a therapeutic activity. He was asked to work a two man saw with another aggressive pattern client. This activity requires cooperation between two people, and also requires that both people learn to physically move away from the partner fifty percent of the time in order to successfully cut through a log. Upon his release from the hospital Mr. Shilmer reported that log sawing had helped him learn to "move back from people" and that this practice had helped him gain significant awareness into "what I do that messes up my relationships with people." He also learned "what I need to do differently."

## Advocacy

Advocacy is an action form of treatment technique which stimulates support through environmental modification. Advocacy includes any activity which helps the client decrease stress by changing the client's social environment (Lantz and Lenahan, 1976). Advocacy can include linking or referring the client to a community resource. It sometimes includes helping the client's social network increase their ability to understand and support the client. Advocacy can also include the therapist's use of his or her authority and prestige to help the client break through bureaucratic red tape which interferes with the client's ability to obtain a needed social resource. Advocacy is most often needed when the client feels overwhelmed by environmental stress, when social institutions are unresponsive to human needs and when the client uses an avoidance pattern as a primary problem solving strategy. Advocacy is a treatment technique most frequently utilized by social workers. In recent years other helping professions have become more knowledgeable about the appropriate use of this treatment technique (Lieb and Slaby, 1975).

## Boundary Setting

Boundary setting is a treatment technique which is most frequently used in family therapy. In boundary setting the therapist helps the family develop a more consistent and effective family communication pattern that places the parents into a family leadership position (Minuchin, 1974) (Andrews, 1979) (Satir, 1967) (Lantz and Thorward, 1985).

In many families the members develop a communication system which includes inappropriate involvement of the children in the parent's marital relationship. For example, a father may become too close to a daughter for emotional nurturance because he is unable to negotiate the meeting of these needs with his wife. The closeness to the daughter reinforces the father's distance from his wife, and the distance from the wife reinforces the inappropriate closeness to the daughter. In such a situation the family therapist will often use boundary setting techniques with the family to strengthen the husband-wife relationship and to help the relationship between the husband and the daughter become less intense (Lantz, 1979). Boundary setting usually occurs experientially during the time and space of the family therapy interview. The following vignette illustrates experiential boundary setting during a family therapy session.

The Morgan family was referred for family therapy by their son's school counselor. The son was having problems at school. The school counselor felt that the family needed help working together so that the family could be more effective in helping the son. In the initial interview the family therapist noticed that the son would do something inappropriate, such as flicking cigarette ashes on the floor, the mother would tell him to stop, and the father would then sabotage the mother by smiling at the son and telling the mother that "it isn't that big a deal." The family therapist assumed that the father was using the son to indirectly express the father's hostility and anger towards the mother. The therapist considered this to be an inappropriate involvement of the son in the parent's marital relationship and decided that boundary setting was an indicated treatment technique. The following conversation then occurred:

| | |
|---|---|
| Son: | (Flicks cigarette ashes on the floor) |
| Mother: | Billy stop that. That's wrong! |
| Son: | (Angry) Get off my back! |
| Father: | (To the wife) Come on Mary, it's not that bad. Get off his back! |
| Son: | (Smiles) |
| | (Family silence) |
| Therapist: | This seems to me to be an excellent example of why the school counselor referred you to family therapy. (To father) I would like you to tell me why you won't support your wife when she tells Billy to stop acting wrong. |
| Father: | Well, I don't think it's that big a deal. |
| Therapist: | It's frequently a very big deal when parents do not work together. It's a very big deal when important people like parents give a kid two entirely different messages. |
| Father: | Well . . . I see your point, but . . . well, she's such a nag. She nags him all the time. |
| Therapist: | (To father) Do you ever feel she nags at you? |
| Father: | (Angry) Yes. A lot. |
| Therapist: | I think that you should start talking to your wife about this directly and that you shouldn't let Billy be the one that tells her how you feel. |
| Father: | So you think I get even with her by not helping her with Billy. |
| Therapist: | I could be wrong but it looks that way to me. Would you be willing to talk about this with your wife? |

After this exchange the husband and wife were able to begin to discuss some of the problems within their marital relationship. The therapist's boundary setting activities helped the son "quit" his job of expressing the father's anger towards the mother.

## Bringing Patterns Alive Within the Interview

Bringing patterns alive in the interview is an intervention technique designed to help the client demonstrate emotional and interactional problems to the therapist, rather than to simply talk to the therapist about these problems (Lantz, 1977) (Yalom, 1983). Such a demonstration is useful as it allows both the therapist and the client the opportunity to observe and understand problems as they occur in the "here and now" rather than in a secondhand fashion. Bringing patterns alive within the interview is an action technique which frequently stimulates the curative factors of experiential validation and insight. The following case material illustrates the use of this action technique.

Mr. Moore requested individual treatment because he had problems making friends, felt socially isolated, and frequently experienced anxiety attacks in social situations. Mr. Moore was a 29-year-old, single male who worked as an accountant. He believed that "people just don't like me" and that "it just happens, I don't do anything wrong." Mr. Moore had very little insight into how he contributed to his social isolation.

When Mr. Moore initially started in individual treatment he had considerable difficulty talking. He felt anxious about the treatment situation and was ambivalent about continuing in treatment. He was usually late for his appointments and would frequently cancel at the last moment. Mr. Moore's pattern of avoiding social contact was manifested experientially in the treatment relationship. Mr. Moore felt that "therapy just isn't working." The therapist believed that it was necessary for Mr. Moore to gain some insight into how his ambivalence and chronic lateness contributed to the isolation he felt with the therapist. The therapist decided to give Mr. Moore feedback about Mr. Moore's behavior during the sessions in a way that would bring these problems alive in the "here and now."

In Mr. Moore's subsequent therapy sessions the therapist directly expressed the therapist's irritation toward Mr. Moore for being late. The therapist told Mr. Moore that the way Mr. Moore was always arriving late felt like he was telling the therapist that the therapist had little value and meaning as a person to Mr. Moore. The therapist expressed his feeling that it was getting harder and harder for the therapist to feel concern about Mr. Moore and his problems. The therapist told Mr.

Moore that this phenomenon of the therapist's diminishing positive feelings was not some "cosmic accident" but was rather directly related to Mr. Moore's behavior toward the therapist during treatment interviews. Mr. Moore was able to use this feedback to get a better idea of how he contributed to his social isolation.

## Cognitive Restructuring

Cognitive restructuring techniques are used to help clients change irrational ideas and beliefs about themselves and their social situation (Lantz, 1978B). Cognitive restructuring techniques are used extensively in rational-emotive therapy. The central idea in rational-emotive therapy is that negative feelings are created by irrational self talk that the person tells the self over and over in a way which both creates and maintains dysfunctional emotion (Ellis, 1962). In cognitive restructuring the therapist uses searching questions, direct advise, and cognitive challenges to help the client change and become more aware of the irrational nature of certain cognitive processes that the client uses to create dysfunctional emotions (Ellis, 1962). Cognitive restructuring techniques are action techniques which can stimulate the curative factors of both experiential validation and insight.

## Dereflection

Dereflection is a treatment technique developed by Victor Frankl (1961) which is designed to help clients learn to move away from people and problems particularly when the person has developed a rigid and inflexible reliance upon either the moving towards or against other people pattern. Dereflection can be particularly useful in family therapy with families that have a member who is suffering with a serious mental disorder such as schizophrenia (Lantz, 1982B). In order to appreciate the appropriateness of using dereflection with such families, it is helpful to summarize some of the recent findings about both the nature of schizophrenia and the types of family interactions that are often associated with schizophrenia.

The schizophrenic client has a core psychological deficit which results in an increased vulnerability to external emotional stress (Anderson, Hogarty and Reiss, 1980). This increased vulnerability may result in part from a biological-chemical disturbance within the receptor sites of the central nervous system (Snyder, 1980). Family interaction with the schizophrenic client is often overly emotional, stressful, and chaotic (Lantz, 1982B). It has not been determined that dysfunctional family interaction creates schizophrenia, or that schizophrenia creates dysfunctional family interaction (Lantz, 1982). It has been determined that the two processes reciprocally influence each other (Lantz, 1982B).

Two major forms of overemotional interaction in schizophrenic families tend to stimulate increased symptomatic behavior in the schizophrenic client: criticism and over-involvement. Decreasing criticism and over-involvement often improves prognosis for the schizophrenic client and may prevent hospitalization or rehospitalization (Anderson, Hogarty, and Reiss, 1980) (Lantz, 1982B).

In this author's experience, overly emotional criticism is often associated with the families hyperintention to "cure" the schizophrenic of his or her symptoms. This hyperintention is generally unrealistic and triggers anger, frustration, and criticism among the non-schizophrenic family members. Emotional over-involvement in the family of the schizophrenic is often the consequence of guilt which is in turn, triggered by hyperreflection about the schizophrenic's problems or the family's possible role in the development of these problems. Both hyperintention to "cure" the schizophrenic and hyperreflection about the schizophrenic process and the family's possible role in this process results in an increased level of emotionality within the family. This in turn is experienced as stress by the schizophrenic because of his or her hypersensitivity to emotionality. As a result the schizophrenic family member will then increase his or her manifestation of symptoms. A vicious circle occurs. Dereflection by the family members in their daily life can decrease family emotionality and help the schizophrenic decrease the manifestation of symptoms. The vicious circle can then be broken, or at least slowed down (Lantz, 1982B) (Lantz, 1986C).

The most practical method to decrease hyperreflection and hyperintention is to help clients direct attention to something else (Lucas, 1981). Three methods of dereflection are particularly useful in helping families of the schizophrenic to think about subjects other than the schizophrenic client: teaching the family about the chemistry of schizophrenia, challenging the family role of "psychotherapist," and helping the family develop nonschizophrenic-connected interests and activities (Lantz, 1982B) (Lantz, 1986C).

The first form of dereflection provides the schizophrenic's family with some basic information about the chemical aspects of schizophrenia. For instance, the dopamine hypothesis of chemical imbalances within the receptor sites of the central nervous system is explained in as clear and simple language as possible. Charts and diagrams are used to explain this theory of causation, and the importance of chemotherapy in the treatment of many forms of schizophrenia. In addition, the family members are told that it is important to help the schizophrenic client stay involved with his or her psychiatrist.

Teaching the family members about the chemical theory of schizophrenia is useful as a method of dereflection because it helps them decrease their feelings of guilt. Hearing that such chemical problems may well exist within the schizophrenic's central nervous system will often help the family members realize that it is not "all our fault." This type of information tends to dramatically cut down the family members' hyper-reflection about the schizophrenic process and their possible role in this process. This dereflection reduces emotionality within the family and has positive benefits to the schizophrenic family member (Lantz, 1982B) (Lantz, 1986C).

Challenging the family role as "psychotherapist" is a second way to reduce emotionality in the client's family. Overemotional criticism of the schizophrenic by other family members is often a result of frustration caused by their unrealistic hyperintention to cure the schizophrenic. To decrease family emotionality it is important to help family members give up their role as psychotherapist." In this method of dereflection the therapist is directive and gives the family members precise guidelines as to which family behaviors are helpful and which are less helpful. In general, family members are encouraged to set up a few simple rules that the client must follow and to tell the client about these rules in a matter-of-fact way. The family members are also encouraged to discontinue highly emotional conversations with the schizophrenic and to avoid arguing about his or her hallucinations and delusions. Such guidelines are often helpful to the family members because it gives them a reason or an excuse to decrease their hyperintention to cure the ill family member (Lantz, 1982B) (Lantz, 1986C).

A third way of dereflection is to help the family develop activities and interests not connected with the schizophrenic client. The therapist guides the family towards enjoyment and meaning found in alternative outlets. Members identify their interests and begin to respond to their home situation in healthier ways.

The Sherman family was referred for mental health services after their 20 year-old son, James, was discharged from a state psychiatric hospital. The son's diagnosis was paranoid schizophrenia and he had experienced nine separate psychiatric hospitalizations between 1977 and 1980. The referring psychiatrist suggested that James' parents should be seen in family therapy because the psychiatrist suspected that "crazy family interaction" was a primary reason for James' constant need for rehospitalization. The psychiatrist felt that if the family therapist could help Mr. and Mrs. Sherman provide a more stable environment for James, he might be able to decrease his need for psychiatric hospitalization in the future.

In the initial family treatment session the parents vacillated between critically blaming James for "all our problems" and blaming themselves for "making our son crazy." The parents were told that neither view was correct. Weekly counseling sessions in which they would obtain more accurate information about the nature of schizophrenia and how to help their son were suggested.

In the first stage of the parent's treatment, they were presented with some basic information about the dopamine hypothesis of schizophrenia and were told that a dopamine imbalance was the primary cause of their son's problems. The parents were also told that this dopamine imbalance most likely made their son highly vulnerable to any emotional stress. The parents were eventually able to make the connection between their son's constant need for rehospitalization and their own overly emotional guilt and blame.

After developing this insight the parents were helped to become less emotional about their son's problems. It was suggested that the first step in becoming less emotional was for them to spend less time reflecting upon their son's situation, or how to "cure" him. The parents were asked to keep a chart to find out how much time they spent each week hyperreflecting about James and engaging in efforts to cure him. Keeping this chart helped the parents realize the disproportionate amount of time and energy they had focused upon their son. They were asked to identify at least five "fun" activities that they could use to replace the time spent on hyperreflection and hyperintention. The parents were directly, actively, and consistently encouraged to "trade in" hyperintention and hyperreflection for "fun" activities. Both parents have reported that this treatment approach has helped them rediscover enjoyment in life. James has not required hospitalization since his parents started this treatment.

## Desensitization

Desensitization is a behavior modification treatment technique used to help people who experience anxiety about a specific stimulus and who then respond to this anxiety by moving away from the anxiety provoking stimulus. The technique of desensitization involves the presentation of the anxiety stimulus to the client at very weak strengths so that the stimulus is not strong enough to elicit the anxiety response (Osipow, Walsh, and Tosi, 1980). The intensity and strength of the anxiety stimulus is then gradually increased until the stimulus no longer triggers the anxiety response even when the stimulus is presented at full strength (Wolpe, 1958). This technique of treatment is based upon the concept of reciprocal inhibitation as presented by Wolpe (1958). Desensitization is frequently useful when working with the avoiding client. This technique stimulates the curative factor of experiential validation.

## Early Recollection Test

The early recollection test is an assessment tool which is particularly useful in the understanding and prediction of human behavior patterns (Lantz, 1980) (Ansbacher, 1947). This technique was first developed and utilized by Alfred Adler (1927) and has been described by Munroe (1955) as being the first form of psychological assessment developed that is today known as the projective test method. In the early recollection test the therapist asks the client to tell the earliest recollection that can be remembered and visualized in his or her mind at the present moment in time. The therapist listens to, and records, the client's feeling of the early recollection to assess the client's present style or pattern of social functioning (Adler, 1927). In other words, the therapist uses the clients telling of the early recollection to determine how the client is doing and living at this moment in time, rather than using the client's telling of the early recollection to determine what has happened to the client in the past.

The use of the early recollection test to determine present human functioning is based upon the Adlerian belief that human perceptions about the past are based in favor of the person's present life style, the person's present feeling state and the person's present life style assumptions (Mosak, 1979) (Lantz, 1980). The Alderian belief is that in the telling of an early recollection, a human being will remember and present only what is in accord with the person's present social functioning style, and that the person will automatically and unconsciously select an early recollection to tell which reveals the person's present style of living (Mosak, 1979). The early recollection test can be used by the therapist to help determine the client's major interactional movement pattern (Lantz, 1980). The following early recollection test was presented by a dependent pattern client. This recollection will then be followed by a similar early recollection presented by an attacking pattern client:

Mrs. Kish:    (Softly) I remember when I was about 4 years old. We were up at the family cottage by the lake and somehow I fell into the lake. I remember very vividly that my father jumped into the lake and rescued me. I remember feeling very upset but then I felt safe.

Mr. Laverte:    (Firm voice) I remember when I was about 6 that I was up at the lake. A kid pushed me in and I had a hell of a time getting out. I remember climbing up on the dock and thinking about how I could get even.

In the first early recollection, Mrs. Kish remembers being upset, being rescued and then feeling safe. Her memory reflects an interactional pattern of being rescued by others and then feeling safe. On the other hand, Mr. Laverte remembers a similar incident of falling into the water, but his memory has a very different feeling tone. He was pushed into the water, he got out of the water by himself, and he remembers feeling angry and then thinking about how he could get even. His early recollection is compatible with the moving against other people's social functioning pattern. An important fact is that both Mr. Laverte and Mrs. Kish chose to remember and tell an early recollection that is compatible and congruent with their present style of social functioning. The early recollection test will frequently provide valuable hints into a client's primary problem solving movement pattern.

## Emotional Accomodation

Emotional accomodation is defined as those internal processes that occur within the therapist that allows him or her to develop empathic understanding for the client system (Lantz, 1980) (Sherman, 1982). Emotional accomodation on the part of the therapist is important because if the client system is to develop new and more functional patterns of social living the client must also give up and change previous dysfunctional patterns (Lantz, Early, and Pillow, 1980). This type of change implies risk. The client will not take such a risk unless the client trusts and feels safe with the therapist. Such initial trust will not develop unless the therapist is able to effectively communicate to the client system a sufficient degree of empathy and concerned understanding (Lantz, 1981) (Lantz and Boer, 1974).

Mimicking behaviors on the part of the therapist often occur after the therapist has developed a sense of emotional accomodation with the client. When a therapist feels concern for the client system the therapist's tone of voice, choice of words, and gestures may begin to take on a few of the client's characteristics (Minuchin, 1974). Mimicking behaviors are often an unconscious or preconscious nonverbal attempt on the part of the therapist to be with and understand the client without losing his or her own autonomy and separateness (Lantz, 1978A). Such mimicking behaviors are generally picked up by the client system on a nonverbal level. This often provides the client with some basis for a beginning sense of trust (Whitaker and Malone, 1953) (Mullan and Sangiulino, 1964). Emotional accomodation is very important in relationship building and stimulates the curative factor of support.

## Experimental Interaction

The technique of experimental interaction is designed to help the client practice and/or experience a new interactional or problem solving pattern. In experimental interaction the therapist gives the client specific suggestions and then asks the client to "try out" a new pattern through implementation of the suggestions. The client is not asked to change his or her basic pattern, but to simply experiment with a new pattern without making any commitment to "lasting change." Such suggestions stimulate less anxiety within the client system because the client is "just experimenting" and is not considered responsible for continuing the change in the future. It allows the client to experience a new method of relating without being "stuck" with the new pattern. The technique should be considered similar to the process of shopping for a new suit or dress in that in experimental interaction the client is "trying on something new" without having to "pay for the merchandise." In this way the technique is respectful of client resistance. Experimental interaction stimulates the curative factor of experiential validation (Lantz, 1978A).

## Fantasy Experiences

Fantasy can be defined as the ability to form a mental picture of an idea, object, or situation that is not actually presented to the senses during the present moment in time (Rabkin, 1977). Fantasy can be used in place of an actual experience to practice a new attitude, feeling, ability, or movement pattern. Fantasy is often utilized in conjunction with relaxation training or hypnosis to intensify the effects of the fantasy experience.

Fantasy is most frequently utilized in clinical social work to help a client practice and experience a new movement pattern. In the following case material, the therapist ues an adaptation of an "ego strengthening fantasy technique" developed by Hammer (1967) to help an avoidance pattern client practice the "moving against" interactional pattern:

Therapist:  (Utilizes a common hypnotic induction ceremony to help the client relax and focus on the therapist's voice.)

Therapist:  Imagine that you are walking in a meadow. The meadow is safe. The sun is shining. You feel warm and secure. On the edge of the meadow is a path through a forest. The path leads to a beautiful waterfall. You want to see the waterfall. As you start to go to the waterfall you notice that the path to the waterfall crosses under a big tree branch. Hanging from the branch is a snake. The snake blocks your path. You are still safe in the warm meadow but you wish to visit the waterfall. The snake blocks your path. Imagine that you become angry at the snake. It is blocking your path and you are angry. You decide to scare it away. Imagine that you start yelling at the snake. You yell at it real loud. You pick up a rock and throw it at the snake. You scare the snake away. You have scared the snake away and the path is open. Imagine walking to the beautiful waterfall and with eash step you take you become more comfortable and happy that you have scared the snake away.

Fantasy experiences seem to be more effective when utilized with individuals who have right brain dominance (Rabkin, 1977). Individuals with left side brain dominance seem to process information in a verbal and qualitative fashion, while individuals with right brain dominance tend to process information in a visual manner (Rabkin, 1977). People who have right brain hemisphere dominance are reported to be more visual, imaginative and more susceptible to hypnosis (Bakan, 1969).

Bakan (1969) suggests that brain hemisphere dominance can often be determined by asking the client to look the therapist in the eye and to then solve a mathematical problem. Often the client will then divert his or her eyes to one side or the other. Such an eye movement is activated by the opposite brain hemisphere which suggests that if the eye movement is to the right than the left side of the brain is dominant. If the movement is to the left, this suggests that the right hemisphere is dominant (Bakan, 1969). Fantasy experiences tend to stimulate the curative factor of experiential validation particularly with clients who have right hemisphere dominance.

## Feedback Methods and Machines

Clients are frequently unaware that they are engaging in behaviors which sabotage healthy and happy human relationships. In many instances behaviors which at first appear to be ingrained will be found instead to be the result of simple ignorance on the part of the client. Feedback from the therapist, or the use of mechanical feedback machines, can help clients understand the unwanted effects of certain client behaviors (Lantz, 1978A). Feedback frequently stimulates the curative factors of insight and experiential validation. In the following clinical example, a mother is able to use feedback to learn that she has been interacting with her children in a verbally abusive manner.

Mrs. Gill, a single parent, requested family treatment because her two teenage daughters were "acting rebellious." Mrs. Gill stated that her daughters were coming home past curfew and were "talking back." She stated that the daughters had developed a "bad mouth." During the first family treatment session Mrs. Gill and the children whined, shouted, blamed, and verbally abused each other. The children felt that the mother was verbally abusive, and the mother felt that the children were verbally abusive. The therapist stated that he believed "you all three sound like a herd of trumpeting elephants." The family interview was being recorded. The therapist stopped the tape recording machine and played back the "family noises" which had been recorded. Both the children and the mother were "shocked" to hear themselves "shouting so loud." All three family members made an agreement with each other to "tone it down." Family therapy proceeded in a much more productive fashion. The mother was particularly effective in monitoring her own "shouting."

## Homework Assignments

Homework assignments can be viewed as task suggestions and recommendations provided by the therapist to extend, expand, reinforce, or promote a change in the clients problem solving patterns after the change has been discussed and/or practiced by the client during the client's treatment sessions. An avoiding client can be given homework that is designed to help the client develop skills in assertive behavior, a dependent pattern client can be given homework that is designed to help the client practice autonomy, and an aggressive client can be given homework that is designed to help the client practice avoidance or dependency. Examples of homework include having a client spend a prescribed amount of time practicing an activity which is incompatible with the client's basic problem solving pattern, having the client read a book which describes or illustrates behaviors that the therapist hopes the client can incorporate into the client's daily life, or having the client keep a diary or journal that can help the client document his/her efforts to learn new problem solving skills. The creative use of homework assignments is limited only by the therapist's imagination and understanding of the client's problems. Homework assignments most frequently stimulate the curative factor of experiential validation.

## Information Giving

It often occurs that the clinical social worker will receive a service request from an individual who has developed anxiety in response to a new situation and/or lack of information about this new situation. In such instances the social worker will frequently be able to document a need for long term intensive psychotherapy. At the same time, and with the same amount of initial information, the social worker will frequently also be able to document a need for the simple provision of new information to the client. This second approach is recommended by the author, when possible, as it tends to save the client a lot of money, and also helps the client avoid the social stigma of having an "emotional problem." The following case material illustrates the appropriate and effective use of short term information sharing in a case that many therapists would consider to be a situation in which long term intensive psychotherapy could be indicated.

Mr. Hamilton called the worker requesting "intensive psychotherapy." He was quite anxious and demanded "an immediate appointment." He was given an "immediate appointment" the following day. The client expressed relief that "something will be done."

In Mr. Hamilton's first appointment he stated that he was upset because he had just found out that "I might be queer." It seems that Mr. Hamilton had been out drinking with some friends and they had inadvertently gone into a gay bar. Mr. Hamilton had been approached by a customer, they had talked and the new acquaintance suggested that Mr. Hamilton was a "repressed homosexual." Mr. Hamilton was very anxious about this suggestion and wanted to "find out if it's true."

The therapist took a fairly complete social history which focused upon Mr. Hamilton's "dating behavior." Mr. Hamilton had never "dated or gone out with a man." He had no memory of "ever getting turned on by a man" and seemed to have a history which strongly suggested a heterosexual developmental pattern. It did become clear that Mr. Hamilton had experienced some minor problems with low self-esteem in the past and at times he had become mildly anxious in new situations. The therapist told Mr. Hamilton that the therapist could find "absolutely no evidence" for the idea that Mr. Hamilton might be a homosexual. The therapist suggested that the "acquaintance" was probably "just hoping." Mr. Hamilton was informed that the therapist believed that "you don't need therapy." Mr. Hamilton was also told that "If you ever need any information again please feel free to call me." The therapist received an announcement of Mr. Hamilton's marriage a few years later. The provision and giving of information frequently stimulates the curative factors of support and insight.

## Interpretations

The clinical social worker views the processes of interpretation in a broader framework than is typically the case in classical psychoanalytical psychotherapy. This process of interpretation has a number of functions in social work practice. These functions include helping the client develop social functioning pattern clarification, helping the client develop the curative factor of insight, and helping the client experience support. It is the author's understanding that the stimulation of insight is the only function of interpretation in the classical psychoanalytical approach. This classical view has been articulated by Kubie (1936).

A major issue which is frequently discussed in the literature written about interpretation is whether or not there is, or should be, a suggestion component included within the interpretation process. Kubie (1936) believes that proper interpretations should be based upon therapeutic objectivity, and that when such interpretations are made in the proper way the process will not include a suggestion component. Other authors (Frank, 1961) (Haley, 1963) (Torrey, 1972) feel that it is impossible to eliminate placebo, suggestion, and encouragement from the interpretation process. Frank (1961) states flatly and clearly that the primary function of an interpretation is to change the client's cognitions in a direction believed to be therapeutic. Frank (1961) points out that even a simple interpretation gives a name or a label to an experience. Such labeling helps the client make sense out of a variety of experiences and in this way increases the client's sense of control and mastery. Torrey (1972) calls this process the principle of "Rumpelstiltskin" because by giving a name to an experience the client can break the experience's power and control.

Both Frank (1961) and Torrey (1972) point out that the process of interpretation is also used by both the therapist and the client to increase the client's sense of trust in the therapist. The therapist can use interpretations to arouse and maintain the client's confidence in the therapist, by providing the client with information which fits, yet explains, the client's situation in a somewhat more optimistic fashion. This increases the client's sense of hope. The following case material illustrates this process.

Ms. Weeks was admitted to a psychiatric hospital for symptoms of depression and suicidal thinking. Ms. Weeks functioned at an above average level of intelligence, yet she believed that she was "retarded" and that she "could not be helped." Her "retardation" existed at an almost delusional level of intensity and represented her primary reason for wishing to kill herself. She believed that she was hopeless because she was "retarded." She was placed in an inpatient psychotherapy group and participated in this group two times a week. In spite of her "retardation" Mrs. Weeks was exceptionally sensitive and very intuitive in her comments about the other group members. The group therapist gave her support for her comments and made the following interpretation. After she had made a particularly insightful comment about another group member, the therapist told Ms. Meeks that "in many ways I believe you are the smartest member of the group; your comments indicate to me that you are an exceptionally intelligent and sensitive human being." The other group members supported the therapist's interpretation and Ms. Weeks suddenly found herself to be without "a very good reason to die." Although initially angry about this turn of events, Ms. Weeks was eventually able to thank both the therapist and the group for their "life giving comments."

An additional effect which can result from the process of interpretation is that the process can be used to both increase and decrease the client's inner state of tension (Frank, 1961). Inner tension seems to be reduced by interpretation which increases the client's sense of mastery, and which increases the client's trust in the therapist. On the other hand, interpretations which confront the client with repressed and unconscious fantasies, feelings, and patterns of behavior tend to increase the client's anxiety because they seem to limit the client's sense of mastery and control. The direction of the interpretation can then be utilized by the therapist to provide a change in the client's level of inner tension. The clinical social worker can utilize this model to pair anxiety and tension with the client's maintenance of a pathological problem solving pattern. The therapist can also use this model to pair a reduction of tension with the manifestation, or emergence, of a more balanced and functional problem solving pattern.

## Maintenance Techniques

Maintenance techniques are defined as including any treatment strategies or behaviors on the part of the therapist which help the client avoid change. Maintenance techniques help the client resist change and therefore they also help the client to remain comfortable. Maintenance techniques can help the therapist promote a therapeutic alliance with the client by minimizing the client's anxiety initially while the client and therapist are getting to know each other (Minuchin, 1974). Maintenance techniques help the client maintain the status quo and as a result the client does not experience the anxiety associated with change. A prolonged use of maintenance techniques create a therapeutic stalemate. The short term use of maintenance stimulates the curative factor of support.

## Mental Status Exam

The mental status exam is generally considered to be a structured way of identifying disturbances in the client's thoughts, feelings, and behavior (Gregory and Smeltzer, 1977). The mental status exam can be useful in identifying signs of both organisity and psychosis. The exam is usually done in the first or second clinical interview and can be done on either a formal or informal basis. The mental status exam should be viewed as an outline which helps the clinical practitioner gather assessment material in a systematic fashion. Such material can then provide hints as to further assessment tools which might be useful and to intervention approaches which might be helpful. The following mental status outline provides one example of the kinds of information which can be obtained in a thorough mental status examination:

A. The Client's General Appearance
   Is the client sad, expressionless, hostile, or worried? Does the client have a flat affect or an inappropriate affect? Is the client's facial expression normal? Is the client's dress normal or abnormal? Is the client's appearance congruent with the client's situation and cultural norms?
B. The Client's Mood
   Is the client anxious, angry, frightened, depressed, labile, manic, or frantic?
C. Motor Activity
   Does the client demonstrate agitation, tics, a tremor, peculiar posture, an unusual gait, or repetitive acts? Does the client demonstrate increased or decreased motor activity?
D. Speech
   Is the client's speech normal or abnormal? Does the client demonstrate slowed, mute, or rapid speech? Does the client stutter?
E. Interview Behavior
   Does the client demonstrate angry outbursts, impulsivity, irritability, hostility, silliness, apathy, withdrawn behavior or evasive behavior? Is the client passive, aggressive, naive, dramatic, manipulative, dependent, demanding, negative, or uncooperative?

F. Perception and Orientation
   Is the client oriented to person, time, and place? Does the client demonstrate or report illusions, hallucinations, or delusions? Does the client experience depersonalization, feelings of unreality, or other sensory disturbances?

G. Thought Processes
   Is the client's flow of thought normal or abnormal? Does the content of the client's thought include antisocial attitudes, assaultive ideas, ideas of persecution, ideas of guilt, ideas of reference, hopelessness, homicidal thoughts, obsessions, suspiciousness, illusions, hallucinations, delusions or phobias? Does the client experience rapid thinking and/or poverty of thought content? Is the client grandiose in thinking and does the client demonstrate overly concrete thinking?

H. Intelligence
   Does the client appear to be above or below average in intelligence? Does the client have a poor vocabulary or a good vocabulary? Does the client use his/her vocabulary in an appropriate way? Is the client impaired in the ability to use abstract thinking?

I. Memory
   Does the client have an intact memory for both recent and past events? Does the client use confabulation to cover a poor memory?

J. Insight and Judgment
   Does the client demonstrate reasonable insight into the reasons for the clinical assessment and/or the purpose of the clinical interview? Is the client motivated for treatment, and is the client realistic about the degree or intensity of his/her problems and symptoms? Is the client realistic about the goals for treatment?

## Modeling

Many clients have not developed effective social functioning patterns because they have never experienced such patterns in their relationships with significant others, or because no one has modeled such a pattern for the client. The therapist can help the client develop increased flexibility within the client's problem solving patterns by providing the client with appropriate models who can demonstrate the desired behaviors for, and to, the client. In many instances, the therapist can be the model. In other instances, the therapist can arrange for the client to observe appropriate models by helping the client contact and connect with socially healthy human beings. At times a well functioning therapy group can be a resource for modeling, and at other times natural social groups within the client's social environment can be tapped for the provision of modeling (Turner, 1978). Modeling often stimulates the curative factors of support, insight and experiential validation.

## Paradoxical Intention

Paradoxical intention is a treatment technique developed by Frankl (1953) which is designed to help anxious clients decrease fear. In paradoxical intention the client is encouraged to do the very thing the client fears. The objective of this technique is to break the vicious circle which results in, and from, anticipatory anxiety (Fabry, 1968). This technique has been found helpful with phobic clients, obsessive-compulsive clients, people who stutter, clients with a sleep disturbance, clients who have sexual problems, and with many other people problems which include an anxiety component (Frankl, 1958). The following case material illustrates the use of paradoxical intention.

Mr. Foxel was referred for therapy by his neurologist because Mr. Foxel was having seizures in a very specific social situation. When making the referral the neurologist explained that Mr. Foxel was epileptic, that his seizures were well controlled on medication, and that the only time Mr. Foxel had seizures was when he had to give a motivational speech at a sales convention. Mr. Foxel was a highly successful sales manager and was requested to give such talks quite frequently. The neurologist hoped that casework might help Mr. Foxel overcome his anxiety and seizures in this specific situation.

In Mr. Foxel's first treatment session he stated that he agreed with his neurologist about the goals for treatment. After talking with Mr. Foxel the therapist felt sure that Mr. Foxel's seizures at "speech making time" were in fact triggered by anticipatory anxiety. The technique of paradoxical intention was fully explained to Mr. Foxel and Mr. Foxel was told that he should try as hard as he could to have a seizure before and during any "speech making activity." Mr. Foxel stated that the technique made sense to him and he agreed to make a speech at the next sales convention. Mr. Foxel later reported that he had solved his problem because "When I try to have a seizure my anxiety goes away and I find it impossible to have one." Paradoxical intention often stimulates the curative factors of support and experiential validation.

## Relabeling

As both Ellis (1962) and Tosi (1974) have noted, many feelings are a direct result of the beliefs and evaluations that people make about themselves and their social situations. Clients often accept a set of cognitive beliefs or myths which must be questioned and/or countered by the worker if the client is to increase his or her capacity for healthy human growth. One strategy for countering dysfunctional cognitive beliefs is the process of therapeutic relabeling (Lantz, 1978B). Therapeutic relabeling is a process in which the worker suggests a new and different evaluation of given phenomenon to the client, which will then result in a more positive human outcome (Zuk, 1972). Relabeling frequently stimulates the curative factors of insight, support and experiential validation. The following segment of a marital therapy session illustrates the process of relabeling.

Wife:       (Angry) I get sick of your excuses and reasons.
Husband:    (Also angry) Excuses hell. If you would stop nagging long enough to listen maybe I could explain.
Therapist:  (Laughs and smiles)
Wife:       (To therapist) What are you laughing about?
Therapist:  I'm just happy that you two care enough about each other to have these fights. I get worried when couples don't care enough to fight it out. That sure is not something to worry about with you guys.

## Ripple Effect Technique

In the ripple effect technique the therapist uses suggestion and tells the client that there is a good chance that if the client is able to successfully solve a specific problem that the client will probably find that he or she will be able to solve similar problems in the future with greater ease. According to Rabkin (1977) and other authorities (Torrey, 1973) the ripple effect occurs more frequently than does symptom substitution. Rabkin (1977) suggests that once the client is mobilized to solve a specific problem the client begins to regain confidence and then finds that it is easier to master other problems.

In the ripple effect technique the therapist uses the client's specific presenting problem as a metaphor to help the client learn how to begin to solve a broader set of difficulties. For example, a client who is avoiding a specific situation may well be able to generalize his or her learning from the successful resolution of the specific situation to other problems when these problems trigger the client's use of an avoidance pattern. The ripple effect can often be magnified through the use of a hypnotic ceremony (Rabkin, 1977). The ripple effect stimulates the curative factors of experiential validation and prestige suggestion.

## Sculpting the Family or the Interactional Situation

Sculpting is a treatment technique that is most often utilized in family therapy. It can, however, also be used in group therapy and in group supervision with mental health professionals. In sculpting, the family therapist, group therapist, or supervision leader asks a member of the family or group to use the other members as "sculpting material" and to build a sculpture or statue of what the interactional situation looks like to the "sculpting member." The sculpting member builds a group statue. When the statue is complete the members of the statue are asked to "hold your positions perfectly still for a few minutes." After a few minutes of staying in a frozen position each member of the statue or sculpture is asked to report "how it feels to be in that position."

In many instances the members of the sculpture will be able to give the sculpting member good feedback about how it feels to be "in this position." Interactional problems are highlighted and at times the client can gain insight into how his or her own interactions help to build a "similar statue in real life." Family sculpting most often triggers the occurrence of experiential validation and insight (Lantz, 1978A).

## Social Interest Tasks

A social interest task is a homework assignment given to a client by the worker which is designed to help the client focus attention away from the self and towards the well being of significant others (Lantz, 1981). Social interest tasks are particularly helpful with depressed clients who see their salvation as coming from the strength of other people. The social interest task challenges the depressed client's view of personal weakness, and reinforces the client's motivation to gain strength through altruistic action. The social interest task assignment stimulates the client's sense of mastery, and gives the client the message that the therapist believes that the client has a set of significant internal strengths which can be shared with other people. Social interest tasks stimulate the curative factors of support and experiential validation. Social interest tasks are particularly helpful with depressed clients who utilize a dependent problem solving pattern (Lantz, 1981). Yalom (1980) believes that such techniques help people to find meaning in their lives.

## Testing

Psychological tests are used to help make clinical decisions, to classify emotional and behavioral problems and to verify scientific hypotheses (Anastasi, 1976). Every psychological test should be selected and used only for the purpose for which it was designed (Osipow, Walsh and Tosi, 1980). Psychological tests should generally only be administered and interpreted by a professional psychologist. A psychological test can be considered to be a way of taking a sample of a client's behavior and then using this sample of behavior to make predictions about future behavior. Such predictions vary in degree of accuracy depending upon the skill of the professional administering and evaluating the test and the validity and reliability of the test instrument that is being utilized (Anastasi, 1976). Psychological testing can be useful in the assessment stage of clinical social work. Such tests can also often help stimulate the curative factor of insight when test results are interpreted to the client by a skilled member of the psychology profession.

## Tracking

Tracking is an assessment tool that is most frequently used in family therapy. In tracking the therapist observes the process of family interaction as it occurs during the time and space of the family therapy interview (Minuchin, 1974). In tracking the family therapist uses his or her observational skills to help determine the intensity and frequency of interactions between family members in the family that is being observed (Andrews, 1974). Tracking can also be done on a more formal basis by charting a sociogram of the interactions that occur between family members (Starr, 1977). Such sociograms can also be utilized in group psychotherapy (Starr, 1977) (Mosak, 1979).

The sociogram method of tracking can be done in two distinct ways. First, the family or group therapist can draw a small circle for each family or group member on a piece of paper, and then use arrows and the directions of the arrows to map out interactional patterns as the family or group members are talking with each other in the "here and now." This method of tracking produces a visual representation of the family interactional pattern.

A second sociogram tracking method is the written test method. In this test each family or group member is asked to choose three other members as companions in a particular life situation fantasy provided by the therapist in the client's order of preference (Starr, 1977). The choices are scored and a diagram can then be produced which outlines the emotional preferences made by each member of the group. Tracking is primarily an assessment tool. At times the therapist can share the results of this assessment tool with the client. At times such sharing stimulates the curative factor of insight.

## Summary

The treatment techniques which have been described are not in themselves curative. A treatment technique is only useful if it stimulates or facilitates the emergence of a natural curative factor. A treatment technique should not be expected to stimulate the emergence of a curative factor unless the technique is compatible with the needs of the client and is used by the therapist in a respectful manner. Any technique will fail to stimulate the desired result when it is utilized in a spirit of manipulation, or when it is used "against the client." There is no treatment technique which can replace the therapist's respect and concern for the client.

## Chapter Three

# TREATMENT MODALITIES

The clinical social worker views the client as a person who is motivated to find a meaningful place in a network of healthy interactions with other significant people (Lantz, 1978A). Although the client's social motivation may well be twisted in a negative direction through fear, anxiety, physical and neurological problems, social stress, or past interactional experience, the client is still always considered to be available for growth. This client availability can be strengthened, reinforced and encouraged through the correct choice of a treatment modality (Andrews, 1973).

Different treatment modalities provide different kinds of growth opportunities. As a result it is important for the therapist to carefully recommend the use of any specific treatment modality. The therapist's recommendations should be based upon a correct assessment of compatibility between the client's needs and the strengths and advantages of the treatment modality which is being chosen. The purpose of this chapter is to describe the advantages, disadvantages, and possibilities for growth found in a number of different treatment modalities.

## Individual Treatment

Individual psychotherapy is a verbal process which occurs between two people; one a therapist and one a client (Sherman, 1982). Individual psychotherapy is in reality a two person group, and in this sense the term individual psychotherapy is somewhat inaccurate.

Individual treatment is the modality of choice when the worker accurately decides that it is necessary and/or important to maximize the therapist's control over the process of treatment. Individual therapy includes two interactional channels; an interactional channel from the therapist to the client, and an interactional channel from the client to the therapist. The individual therapist only has two interactional channels to observe, and the therapist has good control of one of these two interactional channels (i.e. from the therapist to the client). This situation is quite different then in group therapy or family therapy where there is a significant increase in the number of interactional channels which must be observed and where the therapist has less control due to the increased complexibility of the interactional situation. (See figure number three.)

### Control and Support in Individual Psychotherapy

The primary advantage in individual psychotherapy is that the therapist has more control over the process, and because of this control the therapist has an increased ability to set the tone and atmosphere of the treatment interview. The therapist can use his or her interactions towards the client to increase the level of support in a way that in turn decreases the level of anxiety experienced by the client. In group, marital, or family treatment the therapist often loses a considerable degree of such control.

Individual psychotherapy is considered by many authorities (Andrews, 1974) (Schwartz, 1960) to be the least complex form of treatment and the form of treatment which can be most easily controlled by the therapist in order to set up a safe treatment atmosphere. As a result, individual psychotherapy is frequently the treatment of choice with severely disturbed clients, at least in the beginning stage of the client's treatment. The major disadvantage of this modality is that the modality can easily be utilized in a way that distances the client from people within the client's real social network by encouraging the client to develop an overly intense and emotional relationship with the individual psychotherapist (Lantz, 1978A). The nurturance, support, and relationship intensity that is possible in individual psychotherapy is both an advantage and a disadvantage. It can offer continuous and controlled support for clients who need such an experience. At the same time the provision of such support by the therapist can at times inhibit the client from attempting to find such support within the client's natural social network (Andrews, 1979). This disadvantage can sometimes be minimized by utilizing group, marital, and family treatment modalities as an adjunct to individual psychotherapy. The case material which shortly follows (Barbara) will illustrate the use of individual treatment and other adjunctive modalities with a severely disturbed client in a way that maximizes the client's support and still encourages the client to find and develop a personal social network. The clinical material also illustrates

**Figure 3**

**TREATMENT MODALITIES**

INDIVIDUAL THERAPY

GROUP THERAPY

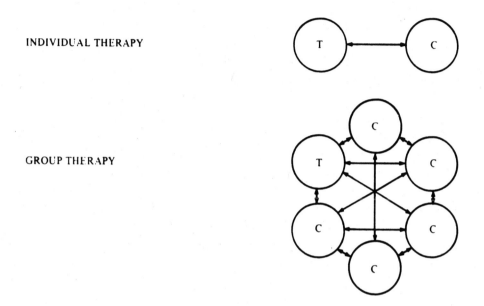

FAMILY THERAPY

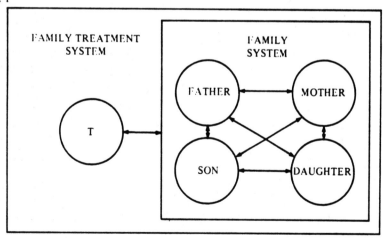

the process of using individual psychotherapy as a primary modality when working with a schizophrenic client in long term intensive outpatient psychotherapy.

## Individual Psychotherapy as a Primary Treatment Modality When Working With a Severely Disturbed Schizophrenic Client

Schizophrenia has been called a physical disease, a dysfunctional style of living, a logical method of existing in an insane world, and an unique psychosocial reaction to stress (Lieb and Slaby, 1975). In recent years many authorities (Lieb and Slaby, 1975) (Snyder, 1980) have concluded that schizophrenia is both a basic biochemical illness and a reaction to stress. In this view it is assumed that the schizophrenic client has a integrative deficit which results in an increased personal vulnerability to stress (Anderson, Hogarty, and Reiss, 1980). This deficit is considered to result from a biochemical disturbance within the receptor sites of the central nervous system (Snyder, 1980). Treatment of the schizophrenic client is generally considered to be most effective when four treatment components are present. These components are: medication, developing a supportive and encouraging treatment relationship with the client, helping the client develop functional lifestyle cognitive assumptions, and helping the client develop useful social living skills (Lantz, 1982B). Specific information about the medications used in the treatment of schizophrenia will not be discussed in this book as it is a subject more fruitfully discussed by practitioners from the medical profession.

## Developing a Supportive and Encouraging Individual Treatment Relationship

Not all helping professionals are ready to develop the kind of relationship necessary when working with the schizophrenic client. The client's bizarre symptoms can trigger intense anxiety reactions in many therapists. Many therapists may handle such feelings by developing inappropriate compensation methods such as hostility toward the client, withdrawal from the client, or expectations that the client improve at a rate that is unrealistic (Lantz, 1984A).

An effective treatment relationship with the schizophrenic client requires that the therapist be able to listen to the client in an active, compassionate way, even if the therapist is unable to understand the content of the client's speech. Sullivan (1946), believes that a clear understanding of the schizophrenic client's communication is not as important as the therapist's respect and willingness to join the client in the client's uncomfortable world. Adler (1927) believes that this approach demonstrates social interest to the client.

A second aspect to the effective helping relationship with the schizophrenic client is flexibility. At times the worker must challenge or confront the client without becoming judgmental, hostile, or disrespectful (Mosak, 1979). The therapist will sometimes need to do things for the client, yet know when to limit this so that the client's ability to grow or become independent is not endangered (O'Connel, 1961) (Lantz, 1984A).

A third aspect of the helping relationship with schizophrenic clients is the therapist's ability to work in a situation that includes few reference points and little stability. The client's ambivalence, confusion, and symptomatic manifestations often result in the therapist's feeling that he or she is on a "shakey boat" in a "rocky sea" with no direction. This experience may result in the development of dogmatic views, the overutilization of certain treatment techniques, or an inflexible attitude (O'Connel, 1961). If the therapist is secure in his or her own sense of self, the therapist generally will not attempt to manipulate the client into providing for the therapist's security. When the therapist does not let his or her anxiety feelings contaminate the treatment situation, provides the client with a secure relationship, provides both stability and flexibility in the treatment situation, and is able to see the client as a human, rather than as a disorganized mental patient, the client frequently will grow, and change (O'Connel, 1961) (Shulman, 1962).

## Helping the Client Develop Functional Lifestyle Assumptions

Schizophrenic clients tend to accept, believe and utilize certain types of cognitive lifestyle assumptions in order to control, predict, and understand psychosocial experiences. Self-concept lifestyle assumptions frequently accepted by the schizophrenic include the idea that the self is inadequate, weak, unacceptable, bad, and socially useless (Shulman, 1962). The schizophrenic also often accepts grandiose lifestyle assumptions about the self-ideal or what the self "should be." Even though schizophrenics maintain a very negative concept of the self, they will still expect the self to be perfect, god-like, and totally superior (Shulman, 1962). As a result, normal human achievement may not have much meaning for the schizophrenic client. The schizophrenic client also frequently develops highly unrealistic ethical standards about right and wrong (Shulman, 1962). Such standards generally are impossible to achieve and as a result the client will develop intense inferiority feelings due to his or her "lack of achievement" in response to such ethical standards. Finally, it should be noted that the schizophrenic client often develops an extremely distorted "picture of the world" (Shulman, 1962). The schizophrenic client generally sees the world as totally unpredictable, continually hostile, and extremely dangerous. This added to the view of the self as inadequate and weak results in anxiety, tension, fear, and the development of psychotic compensation methods used to escape the "impossible situation" (Shulman, 1962) (Lantz, 1984A).

Treatment for the schizophrenic client must include helping the client change distorted lifestyle assumptions. Such a change can result from both experiential and insight treatment strategies. Experiential strategies are both used to "show" the client through "living experience" that the client's "self" does have considerable strength, that the client can develop coping skills that are useful, that the world is difficult but not impossible, and that normal achievement can be accepted, enjoyed, and cherished (Shulman, 1962). Guidance, support, teaching, encouragement, reality testing, and experiential learning are used with the client to help challenge distorted cognitive lifestyle assumptions (Adler, 1927).

Insight strategies are used with the schizophrenic client in the latter stages of treatment. Focusing upon childhood experience and developing too great an interest in insight at too early a stage can play into the schizophrenic's desire to "escape" from the real world and other people by "looking inward." Only after the therapist and the client have established a solid working relationship and only after the schizophrenic client has demonstrated a consistent interest in social living should the worker and client attempt to review the client's past psychosocial experience and how such experience has influenced the development of a psychotic lifestyle. Only at the appropriate time, and only with great care, should interpretation be utilized. With proper timing, such insight strategies can help the schizophrenic client develop a greater understanding of his or her tendency to develop defensive psychotic symptoms as well as a greater understanding of how to prevent such symptoms by instituting alternative social living skills (O'Connel, 1961).

### Helping the Client Develop Useful Social Living Skills

Social living and/or coping skills are a major area of disturbance for most schizophrenic clients. Helping such clients usually requires that the therapist and client spend considerable time working upon improving the client's daily living skills. The therapist may need to teach the client many basic, daily living skills such as how to use a bus, fix dinner, shop for clothing, balance a checkbook, make a doctor's appointment, etc. (O'Connel, 1962) (Lantz, 1984A).

The social interaction skills of most schizophrenic clients usually need improvement. Shulman (1962) notes that the schizophrenic client uses distorted communication as a way of counteracting feelings of inferiority and to put distance between the self and others. Other people often react to such manifestations with anxiety. This is communicated to the client, who experiences more anxiety and increases the use of distorted communication. A vicious circle often results (Shulman, 1962).

In order to help the client improve in this area the therapist must control his or her own anxiety in the treatment situation, help the client learn more useful communication skills in the context of a safe treatment relationship, and help the client gradually learn to apply the newly developed communication skills to other social situations. The following conversation illustrates one way the therapist can help the schizophrenic client develop more useful communication skills experientially during the interview situation:

| | |
|---|---|
| Client: | (With 11 month-old baby crawling on the office floor) Things move fast. |
| Therapist: | What things move fast? |
| Client: | Things. |
| Therapist: | I don't understand. Tell me what things. |
| Client: | The baby crawls a lot and gets into things. |
| Therapist: | Are you comfortable with the baby crawling? |
| Client: | Sometimes one gets nervous. |
| Therapist: | Who gets nervous? |
| Client: | Sometimes one gets nervous. |
| Therapist: | (Softly) Who gets nervous? |
| Client: | I'm nervous about the baby's crawling. |
| Therapist: | That's much clearer to me. Thank you. |

In this illustration the therapist encouraged the client to be more direct and specific in the client's communication. Such experiential learning and encouragement can help the schizophrenic develop more contact with the world and can help the client learn that such contact does not have to be dangerous and/or painful (Lantz, 1980) (Lantz, 1984A).

### A Clinical Illustration: Barbara

The following clinical illustration will be used as a method of illustrating a number of individual treatment concepts and how they can be applied when working with a schizophrenic client. For the purpose of this book I will call the client "Barbara." Barbara is a 35 year-old Caucasian female with no children who comes from an Appalachian cultural background. She has never been married and has no living relatives. I started working with Barbara in 1974, when she was 29. In 1974, Barbara was living in a state hospital setting, where she had been since the age of 17. During that period, Barbara had been released from the hospital on three occasions but each time had failed to stay in the community for more than three weeks. A review of Barbara's hospital record revealed that she had been diagnosed as a paranoid schizophrenic rather consistently during her long hospital stay. At the time of my first contact with Barbara, the hospital staff was skeptical about her chances of making it in the community but wanted to give her the chance by having her utilize a day treatment program for adults which recently had been developed and funded in the community. The release plan for Barbara included chemotherapy, day treatment attendance, financial assistance, an adult foster-home living arrangement at the time of release, and outpatient therapy at a community mental health center. In addition, it was planned that Barbara would start both day treatment and outpatient therapy two months prior to her release from the hospital in order to ease the transition from hospital to community life. At the time of my first contact with Barbara she was taking a very high dosage level of a major tranquilizer and was also on antiparkinson's medication. A self portrait drawing that Barbara did for me in 1974 suggests considerable anger (teeth and mouth), a fear of interacting with the environment (no arms or legs), an extremely poor self-concept (no body trunk), and a psychotic functioning pattern (the extreme distortion of the drawing). In my opinion, the drawing was an accurate reflection of Barbara's psychosocial functioning at that time in her life. After I saw this drawing, I requested that Barbara be given a complete neurological work-up to rule out the possibility of a brain tumor or other serious brain tissue damage. The results of this work-up were negative.

During the first year of treatment, all parties involved with Barbara's treatment focused their attention upon encouraging her to remain in the community and upon teaching her how to live in the community by learning a number of useful living skills. The workers at both Barbara's day treatment program and at her foster home placement all spent considerable time teaching Barbara to ride the bus, how to maintain adequate personal hygiene, how to engage in recreational activities, and other social living skills. Barbara also was seen at least two times a week by her primary therapist (this author) who directed much attention upon teaching Barbara how to verbalize and talk in a "less psychotic" way. This process was identified to Barbara as learning to talk to people in a way that "isn't crazy." The therapist and Barbara agreed to "talk crazy" for part of each session but also to "talk normal" for part of each session.

At the end of the first year of treatment Barbara had learned to cook, ride the bus, bowl, shoot pool, maintain good personal hygiene, and finally to stop "crazy talk" and "talk normal" when she wanted to "get along with people." A second self portrait drawing that Barbara did at the end of the first year of treatment was less disorganized than the first drawing. It included legs, arms, a body trunk, hands and feet. The drawing illustrated the improvement Barbara made during her first year of outpatient treatment.

During the second and third years of treatment Barbara remained on medication, continued to live at the foster home, and continued individual therapy and day treatment. In addition, Barbara joined an ongoing outpatient treatment group that was facilitated by this author. The focus of this group was to help group members identify and change dysfunctional lifestyle assumptions and dysfunctional interactional methods. Barbara was able to use this group to help her identify inferiority feelings and to help her identify how to cope and/or handle these feelings without distorting reality. She learned to "check out her feelings without distorting reality." She learned to "check out her feelings with others," to "ask for support," and to "tell people when she was feeling paranoid" before she needed to distort reality. Barbara also learned through experience that other people are not necessarily "dangerous" and that living "in the world" can be an enjoyable activity. At the end of Barbara's third year of treatment she produced another self portrait drawing. Again, a comparison of this drawing with previous drawings illustrated Barbara's continued improvement. During Barbara's third year of treatment her medication was decreased significantly by the agency psychiatrist.

During the fourth, fifth and sixth years of treatment Barbara stopped attending day treatment and found a job. She moved from her foster home placement into her own apartment. She no longer used financial aid. She joined a social club at a local YWCA and continued individual treatment with this author. In addition, the psychiatrist involved in Barbara's treatment continued to decrease her medication. When her primary therapist (this author) went to work at a different agency during the fourth year of treatment, Barbara decided to follow and receive treatment services at the author's new agency.

At the beginning of Barbara's fourth year of community treatment, both Barbara and her therapist began to examine and reflect upon how Barbara's childhood experience had contributed to her psychotic style of living. In addition, considerable time and effort was put into helping Barbara identify, challenge, and change those dysfunctional lifestyle assumptions that had helped create her inferiority feelings and psychotic compensation methods.

Barbara is still in outpatient treatment. She is being maintained on a very low level of medication. She works full time, remains socially active, says that she has not hallucinated or become delusional in over three years, is involved as a big sister volunteer at a local social service agency, has purchased and paid for a car, and has completed high school equivalency training. Barbara also attends technical school part time in the evenings and hopes to become a practical nurse. Barbara remains in treatment with this author. Some work still needs to be done.

Barbara's treatment illustrates the use of individual therapy as a primary treatment modality and also demonstrates the adjunctive use of other modalities in combination with individual psychotherapy. The clinical illustration also provides a fairly accurate description of long term individual psychotherapy with an extremely disorganized schizophrenic client. Individual treatment was useful to Barbara because it gave her a primary, continuous, and reliable supportive relationship over a very long period of time.

### Individual Psychotherapy as a Somewhat Sterile Treatment Field

Although the primary advantage of individual treatment is that it can provide the more disturbed client a reliable and supportive relationship over a lengthy period of time, the modality also has other highly important treatment advantages. Another advantage is that the modality provides the therapist and the client with the opportunity to develop a treatment relationship that is not highly contaminated by outside influences such as having the client share the treatment relationship with other individuals who are a part of the client's natural social network (Kubie, 1936) (Freud, 1933) (Basch, 1980). This advantage has been called the sterile field advantage (Torrey, 1972), and it allows both the therapist and the client to view many of the client's dysfunctional patterns which are directed towards the therapist as representative difficulties which the client brings to the individual treatment situation. In this view, the client is considered to be stuck in the use of a particular dysfunctional pattern or set of defense mechanisms which are not appropriate or useful in his or her relationship with the therapist. This gives the therapist and the client a great opportunity to analyze both the compulsivity and reasons for the client's use of a dysfunctional pattern. In classical analytic psychotherapy this form of discussion with the client is called a transference interpretation (Kubie, 1936). In casework this form of discussion is often called pattern clarification (Turner, 1978) (Hollis, 1972).

Pattern clarification can be heightened in individual psychotherapy because the client is only dealing with the therapist and is not forced to deal with any additional significant others as is the case in marital, group, or family treatment. Outside influences are minimized in individual psychotherapy, and dysfunctional patterns can be highlighted due to the absence of external stimulation. The following clinical material illustrates this process:

Client:　　　(A dependent pattern client) Here are some blank insurance forms that you need to fill out. (Client places the forms on the therapist's desk.)

Client:　　　They need to be filled out right away.

Therapist:　(Picks up the forms) I notice that you did not fill out any of the parts that you are asked to complete.

Client:　　　Well you have all that information, you can do it.

Therapist:　Yes, I can do it, but this is also something you can do, and I believe our agreement is that you would be filling out the section that the insurance company asks the client to fill out.

Client: Well . . . I just thought that you could fill it out. I don't know . . . it just seemed that you could do it.

Therapist: This may well be another example of the pattern we have been talking about for a couple of weeks now.

Client: You mean about me feeling weak and trying to get other people to protect me.

Therapist: (Silence)

Client: Like I can fill them out myself so why would I try to get you to do it.

Therapist: (Silence)

Client: (Silence)

Client: You're right. I know what our agreement is, and I can fill the forms out. I just feel better when people do these little things for me. I don't know, it gives me confidence.

Therapist: Confidence?

Client: It's crazy, when I get people to do these things I feel comfortable, yet I get angry because I think they don't respect me . . . you know they think I'm weak.

Therapist: And what do you end up feeling about yourself?

Client: That I'm weak.

Therapist: I think that there is a difference between comfort and confidence.

Client: It's a move I make on myself to keep me believing I am weak. I just keep doing it and . . . well it's like it pays off . . . I get out of a lot of things but . . . it makes me feel weak.

Therapist: So you pay a price.

Client: Yea, I pay a price. It makes me weak.

The previous conversation may initially appear to be a simple argument between the client and the therapist about who will fill out a section of an insurance form. A closer look reveals that the client has brought to the clinical situation a particular style of problem solving. This style is to depend upon others to solve difficulties that in fact can be solved by the client himself. Treatment can be viewed as a problem solving process where the client and the therapist work together to solve a problem brought to the treatment situation by the client. The general pattern of how the client uses, or attempts to use, the therapist can be extremely revealing in terms of highlighting the client's overall style of social living. The individual treatment situation can be very useful in such an assessment as the lack of complexity (i.e. the sterile field) in itself can magnify the client's use of a primary problem solving pattern. The client's ability to deny this pattern and/or to externalize the responsibility for the pattern is also minimized.

### Individual Psychotherapy as Encouragement for Internal Reflection

Although at times the individual treatment situation can discourage the client's ability or desire to solve problems in the real world by encouraging too much internal reflection, this disadvantage can at times also become a real advantage. Some clients have developed a pathological focus upon external and/or situational aspects of social living. Such clients often have little awareness of their own feelings, goals, thoughts, responsibilities, fantasies, or expectations. Such clients have been labeled by Arieti (1955) as clients who "live for the dominant other." These clients develop a constricted idea of the self and view the meaning of their own life and feelings as less important than the life and feelings of other people. Such clients usually benefit greatly from a type of treatment that "introduces the client to the self." Such an introduction is encouraged and reinforced by the individual treatment modality as this modality is the modality par excellence for internal reflection and the development of internal self awareness (Sherman, 1982). The following case material illustrates this advantage in individual treatment:

Client:      Last night my husband was so upset about his income tax. He didn't eat and went to bed early.

Therapist:   (Silence)

Client:      He was upset and well, I don't know what else was bothering him.

Therapist:   What did this situation mean to you?

Client:      Well, that he was upset and angry, and well . . . he was just upset.

Therapist:   What were your feelings in the situation?

Client:      Just that he was upset. He works so hard and this additional bill was upsetting for him to find out about.

Therapist:   You do a very good job telling about your husband's feelings but I feel left out about your feelings in response to the situation. Your husband is not even with us but you tell me only about him. I end up feeling concern for your husband. I have absolutely no idea about how you are feeling. I don't want to leave you out of my concern.

Client:      Well I don't feel particularly important.

Therapist:   Last night or now?

Client:      (Silence)
Therapist:   (Silence)
Client:      Well I was upset too. He gets upset, and then I feel guilty.
Therapist:   I would like to hear about your guilty feelings. Could you
             help me understand more about this.

In this clinical situation the therapist pointed out to the client that she was talking exclusively about her husband and leaving out information about her feelings. The therapist pointed out that the husband was not even present, yet the therapist was only feeling concern for the husband. He was also feeling in danger of leaving the client out of his concern. The context of the individual interview helped the client to focus upon her own feelings. If the husband had been present there is an excellent chance that the client would have had even greater difficulty revealing her feelings. The structure of the modality helped the client focus in an internal direction.

### Group Therapy

Group therapy is often the treatment modality of choice when attempting to help clients change interpersonal patterns of behavior (Yalom, 1970). The group therapy modality is useful with a wide variety of clients and problems. It can be used with children, adolescents, young adults, older adults, inpatient clients, outpatient clients, neurotic clients, psychotic clients, character disorder clients, clients with organic central nervous system damage, substance abuse clients, growth oriented clients, and with many other client populations (Yalom, 1970) (Andrews, 1972).

The therapy group gives the client the opportunity to have an emotional and significant relationship with both a therapist and with other members of the treatment group (Wolf and Schwartz, 1971). The client can receive both support and confrontation from the therapist or co-therapy team and also from the other members of the treatment group. Yalom (1970) notes that a number of learning opportunities are available to the group therapy client which might not always be available if the client is utilizing a different modality. Such learning experiences can include installation of hope, universality, imparting of information, altruism, the corrective recapitulation of the primary family group, the development of socializing techniques, imitative behavior, catharsis, cohesiveness and interpersonal learning (Yalom, 1970).

It is the author's preference to utilize family and/or marital therapy when the client's problem seems specifically related to the family or marital situation. If the client is having problems in both the family and outside of the family situation, some combination of individual, group, and family treatment is often indicated. Group therapy is frequently indicated with a child, adolescent, or adult who is not living in a natural family group, or who lives in a natural family group that is not willing or able to support and encourage client change. Group therapy is also highly recommended for emancipated adults who need to replace old patterns which were once found to be useful in the family of origin, but which create difficulties for the client in his or her life away from the original family group. Family therapy tends to reinforce closeness within the family. Group therapy can be used to stimulate autonomy and emancipation from the original family group when this is developmentally appropriate (Andrews, 1973).

## Heterogenous and Homogenous Groups

Placing a client into a therapy group increases the complexity of the client's treatment situation (Andrews, 1972). (See figure number three.) The client is forced to relate to both the therapist and a variety of different group members who also have problems. The client becomes one of many, and the worker must be able to observe and understand a great number of group transactions as they occur during the group therapy interview. Increased complexity decreases the amount of control that the therapist has over the process of treatment. At the same time it can also provide the therapist considerable help from the other group members in terms of giving the client additional support and confrontation (Yalom, 1970).

The process of group therapy is greatly enhanced by effective group membership selection (Lantz and Boer, 1974). To some extent the therapist can guide the process of the group by the selections the therapist makes in determining group membership. Membership selection can be done in a way that results in a homogenous group, a heterogenous group, or a group which includes a balance of heterogenous and homogenous elements (Slavson, 1951) (Andrews, 1972) (Andrews, 1965).

A homogenous group includes members who have similar problems and characteristics. For example, the members may be people who live in the same kind of neighborhood, who are approximately the same age, the same sex, and who utilize similar problem solving patterns. Homogenous membership selection attempts to place members in the group who are similar. Sameness is planned and reinforced. The advantage of the homogenous group is that it maximizes the support that each group member feels from the other group members. The homogenous group minimizes the amount of confrontation that is included in the process of the group. A primarily supportive group atmosphere is always encouraged by homogenous membership selection (Slavson, 1951).

A primarily heterogenous group includes members who are different from each other. Such differences can include differences in age, sex, race, social and economic status, and problem solving patterns. Encouraging differentness in the composition of a group increases the level of confrontation that occurs during the group. An increase in confrontation improves each member's opportunity to experience a different point of view, yet this increase in confrontation also decreases the supportive component (Slavson, 1951) (Andrews, 1972).

In the balanced group therapy situation the therapist selects members for the group in a way that ensures that both heterogenous and homogenous elements are present in the group membership composition (Andrews, 1965). A balanced group therapy membership composition maximizes the occurrence of both support and confrontation during the ongoing process of the group (Lantz and Boer, 1974).

It has been the author's preference, in order to ensure the presence of both support and confrontation, to pick at least two group members who can comfortably utilize an aggressive problem solving pattern, two members who can comfortably use a dependency pattern and two members who use an avoidance pattern. Including two group members who can utilize each of the three major problem solving patterns provides each single group member with support from at least one other group member who also utilizes a similar pattern. At the same time this selection approach also provides each group member with the probability of obtaining confrontation from at least one other group member who uses a different problem solving pattern and who will be uncomfortable with the first group member's primary pattern. Such group membership composition provides each group member with an opportunity to negotiate a relationship with another group member who shares the client's pattern and the opportunity to negotiate a relationship with another group member who does not share the client's problem solving pattern (Andrews, 1965) (Lantz and Boer, 1974).

It is also the author's group selection preference to include at least two group members in the group who share certain demographic characteristics such as income level, sex, race, and age. For example, it is not considered advisable to place just one elderly client into a therapy group with younger adults (Andrews, 1972). It is considered safe to place two elderly adults in such a group. The second approach ensures that the elderly client will have at least one other group member who can be considered similar and supportive, at least in the dimension of age. It is generally considered inappropriate to place a client into a group without there being at least one other group member who can identify with the client about the client's age, sex, race, or income level (Lantz and Boer, 1974). When this is not properly planned it often results in scapegoating (Andrews, 1972).

## Group Therapy Treatment Goals

A prerequisite to attending the first group therapy session is the client's verbalization of a contract or a decision about a general goal for personal change (Lantz and Boer, 1974). It may take several individual sessions with the client before the client can verbalize such a general goal for change. Examples of such a contract include "I want to learn to control my temper," "I want to learn how to listen to people and to be concerned about people," "I want to find out why I don't have any friends and how to change this," "I want to learn to be more aggressive," "I want to learn to convince people that I am not a doormat," and "I want to learn how to talk with people without getting scared to death." Placing a client into a therapy group without the establishment of a contract can result in a dead group where little happens and discouragement spreads rapidly (Lantz and Bōer, 1974). The contract can initially be a general contract. A more specific contract can occur at a later point in time.

## Relationship with the Group Therapist

All group members should have a relationship with the group therapist before the client enters the group situation (Andrews, 1965). This is important as there is always a great deal of anxiety associated with group membership, at least in the beginning stage. The client needs a preexisting relationship with the worker in order to handle this anxiety (Lantz and Boer, 1974). This preexisting relationship with the therapist provides support and allows the client to proceed with relating to the other group members. As opposed to the family therapist or the marital therapist who may need to spend a great deal of time and energy getting into the preestablished family system, the group therapist is in on the ground floor in developing group norms (Yalom, 1970). This ground floor is the therapist's preexisting relationship with each group therapy member (Andrews, 1965).

## Group Task Orientation

Group task orientation refers to the process of teaching group members how to use the group experience in a helpful way (Andrews, 1972). This is initially the responsibility of the group therapist. As the group develops maturity, experienced group members can start to help newer members learn how to use the group.

Group task orientation includes the presentation of clear messages from the therapist about the goals of the group, general group rules and some of the specific ways each group member can personally use the group to develop more useful social living patterns.

## Empathy in Group Therapy

Empathy refers to the process of attempting to understand the client and to have some awareness and concern for the client's pain (Lantz, 1978). Empathy does not mean overidentification or the process of confusing our own experience with the experience of another person. Empathy is an active process. Empathy helps people feel better, not because it results in total understanding, but rather because it demonstrates our interest and concern. Again, the group therapist has the primary responsibility to demonstrate empathy during the initial stages of the group. As the treatment group develops maturity, clients will take on the empathy function as they learn to replace overidentification with an active attempt to care for each other in a way that includes an acceptance of differences (1984B). In this way empathy stimulates the replacement of grandiose self ideal expectations with an acceptance, emergence and support of the participant's real self (Lantz, 1984C).

## Interpretation in Group Therapy

Interpretation in group therapy refers to the process of using verbal feedback to help a client in the group develop improved insight into his or her social functioning patterns and/or the developmental antecedents for these patterns. In addition, interpretations are particularly useful in helping the client develop more awareness of inaccurate symbolizations which create negative emotions and identity loss feelings. Interpretations can be made by the group therapist and/or by clients participating in the group. Heterogenous group balance helps the group as a treatment unit provide more accurate interpretations, where homogenous group balance increases the risk of inaccurate group interpretations based upon overidentification.

Effective group membership selection, the articulation of a reasonable group treatment goal by each member, a preexisting relationship with the group therapist, a realistic group task orientation, effective group empathy and accurate group interpretations are all variables which significantly help each group member's experience to be helpful (Lantz and Boer, 1974) (Lantz, 1984B). The following clinical material illustrates an effective adolescent therapy group in which the group members are able to provide for each other a balanced amount of both support and confrontation:

| | |
|---|---|
| Ted: | (An aggressive pattern client) Like there is only three people in this group that's got any brains: Jim, Ann and Carol. They got some smarts (Jim and Ann are the co-therapists). |
| Jack: | (An aggressive pattern client) (Angry) Are you saying I ain't got any brains? |
| Ted: | If the shoe fits, wear it. (Laughing) |
| Al: | (Dependent pattern client) That's not what he's saying. What he's saying is that these three are better than him. |
| Carol: | (Dependent pattern client) Right. He put himself down too. He didn't include himself. |
| Ann (Co-Therapist: | So you think he put himself down? |
| Ted: | How? |
| Al: | By saying that there were only three people with brains and then leaving yourself out. |
| Ted: | (Excited) Yea, but Ann and Jim went to college and all that, and like they're over there all cool and everything |

|  |  |
|---|---|
|  | and like we're all here ... depressed and everything. So that means they got some brains. (Silence) |
| Ted: | Well everyone got some brains really. |
| Jim (Co-Therapist): | How about Ted? (Silence) |
| Jack: | Well? |
| Ted: | (On the verge of tears) Well, my mother, she's always saying I'm a dumb nigger with no brains and I'll never be nothing but a dumb nigger. |
| Al: | So cause your mother says you're dumb that means it's true? |
|  | (Silence) |
| Al: | Well? |
| Ted: | (Softly) No. |
| Al: | Well, like your mother's got some problems so like why listen to her about that. You know you're not dumb and crazy. Just because she puts you down doesn't mean you got to put yourself down too. Nobody in here thinks you're dumb. |

In this excerpt, Ted (moving against), attempts to put himself one-up by complementing the cotherapists and putting down the group. Jack (moving against), accepted the put-down and became angry. Al (moving towards), looked beyond the put-down and commented upon the feelings behind Ted's maneuver by saying that Ted had also put himself down. Carol (moving towards), also picked up on Ted's underlying feelings. The group was able to confront Ted with his actions, his negative feelings about himself, and to also give him some support and acceptance. The group treatment climate included both support and confrontation, accurate empathy, effective and accurate group interpretations and a therapeutic group task orientation.

## Growth Stages in Group Treatment

The purpose of this section of the chapter is to introduce a number of growth stages identified by Quaranta (1971) as these stages relate to the experiential component in group treatment. The group therapist can use this growth stage model to help provide direction and clarity in the complex group therapy treatment process. The model can also be used to help identify useful intervention strategies as well as to help determine the proper timing of such interventions. The six growth stages identified by Quaranta (1971) are the awareness stage, the exploration stage, the commitment stage, the skill development stage, the skill refinement stage and the redirection stage.

In the awareness stage the therapist helps the group members gain some initial understanding that the development and/or continuation of personal symptoms is, at least in part, a result of the problem solving patterns between each client and his or her social network (Lantz, 1984C). In this stage the therapist helps the group participants operationalize their patterns experientially within the time and space of the group therapy interview. After a few such patterns have been manifested during the group, the therapist invites all group participants to observe these patterns and attempt to understand how group members contribute to the continuation of these patterns. Specific techniques utilized by the therapist in this stage can include: pattern prescription, the bringing alive of symptoms and past interactions in the interview room by the use of role of playing activities, and feedback from the therapist to the group members about what the therapist sees occurring between group members during the interview (Boer and Lantz, 1974) (Andrews, 1972).

The end of the awareness stage is frequently characterized by the occurrence of the following behaviors: there will be a significant increase in resistance to the idea of the members meeting as a group, participants will generally feel less comfortable about being in the group, and group members will increasingly look to the therapist for direction in terms of what behaviors to exchange for previously used patterns.

The ending of the awareness stage is the most critical point during the client's participation in group therapy. With an increase in awareness, there is often also an increase in the amount of pain experienced by the participant. Previously used patterns are no longer as effective in the covering of identity loss feelings, and group participants have not yet developed alternative patterns. It is a time when the therapist must offer a great deal of support. The therapist must also help direct the group members into new patterns that can replace the old. This occurs by moving into the exploration stage.

In the exploration stage of group treatment the therapist attempts to engage group members in a process of problem solving experimentation (Lantz, 1984C). The therapist wants to help the members discover through exploration, a number of different social living possibilities that the members can experience as alternatives to older patterns. In this stage the therapist uses direction, suggestion, and encouragement to provoke the occurrence of specific pattern changes. To a member who frequently avoids conflict and contact, the therapist might say, "Tell another member how that feels to you; they may not know." A group member who wants, but is afraid to ask, for support can be told, "So ask for a hug if that's how you feel." The goal in this stage is to help each participant discover that there are more enjoyable and functional social living alternatives that can be added to the old patterns.

Towards the end of the exploration stage, group members will often feel a sense of excitement. New social living possibilities have been identified and experienced, and there is often an increase in the client's sense of hope. It is important to note that this hope will be short-lived unless the client can move into the commitment and skill development stages.

During the commitment stage the client, having identified and experienced a few more functional social living patterns, is asked to make a decision to either terminate their participation in group treatment or to continue working on basic and lasting social living change (Lantz, 1984C). Such a specific decision cannot always be made until the group members have gone through both the awareness stage and the exploration stage. Without sufficient awareness, the group members will not know that change is either necessary or desirable. Without having explored and experienced social living alternatives, the members will not know that change is possible, and the group members will have little specific understanding of the direction in which change could or should occur. Pressing the group members for a commitment to specific change prior to the completion of awareness and exploration is somewhat like asking an individual to like spinach or ice cream before the individual has ever taken a taste. With the completion of awareness and exploration, the group participants can make a more intelligent and informed decision towards either commitment or termination.

If group members make a commitment for continued change, they will then move into the skill development stage. In this stage group members attempt to identify and practice specific problem solving alternatives that will be successful additions to their present social functioning style. The skill development stage is a time of repetition, practice, hard work, and a recognition by group members that they must replace magical expectations of immediate success with the process of consistent work directed towards hard fought therapeutic gains (Lantz, 1984C).

Skill development can occur experientially within the time and space of the group interview. In this process the therapist points out to group members the old patterns that continue to re-emerge, as well as specific alternatives which can be used to replace these old patterns. Skill development can also occur when the therapist or group assigns group members various homework assignments. A third method of skill development is practice for the future. In this process the therapist sets up a fantasy situation in which the group members can practice solutions to social living issues that may become troublesome in the future.

In the skill refinement stage the group members continue to practice the recently learned, more functional social living skills. In this stage the group members are usually willing to change their own behavior when representative social living problem emerge within the group. Projection and blame are replaced by responsibility and maturation. In this stage the therapist takes a less active role, allowing the group members themselves, the opportunity to more actively direct the continued refinement of their own newly developed social living alternatives.

The redirection stage occurs as group members are getting ready for termination (Lantz, 1984C). In this stage the group members are committed to the use of new social living methods and patterns. The members have significantly changed dysfunctional patterns and most importantly, they have learned how to talk with other members and other people about social living issues in a way that allows them to generate new solutions as new problems arise (Lantz, 1984B). In the redirection stage, the therapist helps the group members celebrate change. Redirection is complete when the individual group member, the therapist and the other group members terminate their relationship. The termination is an affirmation by the therapist and the group of the individual group members' continuing ability to grow.

## Case Illustration

Linda is a forty-one year old married female who requested admission to a psychiatric hospital because she was feeling depressed and suicidal. At the time of admission Linda complained of energy loss, crying spells and suicidal feelings. She reported that she had been feeling depressed for about one year and that her depression "just keeps getting worse."

Linda had been placed on an adequate level of antidepressant medication by her family doctor six months prior to her admission to the hospital with no positive response. Linda stated that she first started feeling depressed after her youngest child left home to get married. The feelings of depression deepened at the time of her youngest child's first marital anniversary which occurred three weeks prior to her admission to the hospital. Linda stated that "I'm suffering from the empty nest problem." Her treatment program at the hospital included individual and marital therapy, the stopping of her antidepressant medication and group therapy two times a week.

In the awareness stage of Linda's group therapy experience she informed the other group members that she "needed to be needed." These feelings were demonstrated in the group by her frequent "mothering" of other group members at the expense of her own feelings and needs. Linda was confronted by some of the more experienced group members who told her that they felt her mothering was "phoney" and it was designed to help her and not really to help other people. The members reported that they would like her help but that they didn't trust the help of "anyone who couldn't help herself first." Although such confrontations were painful, Linda was able to make an agreement with other group members that she would "try out some new ways to feel better other than being the group mother."

During the exploration stage Linda began experimenting with using the patterns of directly asking for support and using self-reliance. She had difficulty with these two alternatives and since she was not using her original pattern of "mothering" she began to more fully and directly experience her identity loss feelings. She became more aware of her low self-concept, her high self-ideal expectations and her distrustful picture of the world. With help and support from the group and with the group's positive response to Linda's attempts at self-reliance and directly asking for help, Linda began to change. She started to question her low opinion of herself and her high expectations for herself. She decided that the other group members really were "trustable."

During the commitment stage, Linda decided to "really change." She further outlined her goals for the group being "to find out who I really am, learning to like myself, learning to stick up for myself, and learning to trust other people." These goals were compatible with the hospital's treatment plan.

In the skill development and skill refinement stages of Linda's group therapy experience, Linda used the group to learn as much as she could about her own real strengths. She also used the group to practice a variety of different methods of both directly asking for support as well as supporting and encouraging herself.

After sixteen weeks of inpatient group therapy Linda terminated treatment and left the hospital. In her last few group therapy sessions Linda celebrated the changes she had made. She also requested a referral to an outpatient treatment group. Seven months later Linda called her inpatient group therapist to report that she, her husband, her son and her new daughter-in-law had had an excellent time "out on the town" celebrating "the second anniversary." There has been no reoccurrence of Linda's depression.

## Marital and Family Treatment

The central idea in marital and family treatment is the assumption that most emotional problems are initiated, reinforced, and/or supported by the family or marital system context in which these symptoms and problems occur (Andrews, 1974) (Andrews, 1979). Family and marital systems are composed of reciprocal, interlocking relationship patterns which can have a profound influence upon the behavior, feelings, and attitudes of the individual family members (Andrews, 1983) (Lantz, 1978A). The individual within the family who exhibits a symptom can be considered as a "symptom carrier" or "identified patient" who signals that there is a major disturbance within the total family group or marital system (Satir, 1967) (Andrews, 1973) (Lantz, 1985A) (Lantz, 1985B).

Marital and family therapy treatment modalities shift the focal point of evaluation and intervention from simply the individual in pain to the person's total network of significant interpersonal relationships (Lantz, 1986B) (Lantz, 1986C). A primary goal in these two modalities is the alteration of dysfunctional interactional patterns existing within the marriage or family which supports symptoms in self-perpetuating, causal cycle (Andrews, 1979) (Lantz, 1977).

For example, Mrs. Sonberg requested treatment from a mental health center for her son who refused to go to school. She stated that when she took her son to school he would become ill. She would then take him home. Mrs. Sonberg was given an appointment to see a family therapist. She, her son and her husband were all asked to come to the first treatment session.

During the initial family interview it became apparent that Mr. and Mrs. Sonberg had developed a somewhat distant relationship with each other over the last few years. Mr. Sonberg reported that he worked long hours and that he enjoyed being away from home as he viewed Mrs.

Sonberg as "always feeling depressed." Mrs. Sonberg reported that she felt sad and alone and did "hate to face the day without my son." In this clinical situation the son stopped getting sick at school as soon as mom and dad started spending more time together. It is not entirely clear whether the son's sudden improvement was reactive to his relief at finding his parents back together again, or whether he simply went to school because mom was able to insist now that she again had her husband's support. What is clear is that the son's "school phobia" was in fact signaling a problem within the total family system.

### The Family as a System

The family can be defined as a natural relationship system which has both a history and a future (Lantz, 1977). In this system each individual member of the system has an influence upon all other members and every other member, in turn, has an influence upon each individual member. This process of mutual influence within the family is considered by most authorities (Satir, 1967) (Andrews, 1979) to be a powerful reinforcement system which is often called reciprocity (Lantz, 1979) (Andrews, 1979).

Reciprocity can be defined as a process in which the relationship members reinforce their own and each other's problem solving style (Lantz, 1979). If the interactions and behaviors which are being reinforced are functional, then the process of reciprocity is functional. If the interactions being reinforced are dysfunctional, then in such instances, the process of reciprocity is also dysfunctional (Lantz, 1985A). A large percentage of the therapist's energy in marital and family treatment is directed toward interrupting and challenging dysfunctional reciprocity which inhibits family growth (Andrews, 1974) (Lantz, 1985B) (Andrews, 1979).

### The Family Therapist as an Outsider

Family therapy is similar to group therapy in that both modalities are considerably more complex than is individual treatment. There is, however, one major difference between group therapy and family therapy. In group therapy the therapist has a preexisting relationship with every member of the group. The therapist knows every member, at least as well as the member is known by all the other group members. This is not true in family therapy (Lantz, 1986A). In family therapy every individual family member knows more about the history and operation of the family group than does the therapist. The family members live with each other, have a great influence upon each other, know each other's history and secrets, and also spend a great deal more time with each other than they do with the therapist. The therapist is, and remains, somewhat of an outsider (Lantz, 1986B) (Lantz, 1986C). (See figure number three.)

Although the family may well want help, many families will also resist help. This is true for a variety of reasons, but one important reason is that family change is usually accompanied by family anxiety. This anxiety can be removed by simply defeating the family therapist's efforts to facilitate change. Whenever the family system experiences too much anxiety (too much for them) the family members will join together (i.e. drop their differences) and systematically defeat the therapist. The family group members will be able to do this because of their history, future, and dependence upon each other. This does not happen frequently in group therapy because the group members do not have a past relationship with each other, and because the therapist is an insider. As a result, timing of intervention becomes even more important in family therapy than in group therapy because of the family's ability to join together to defeat and expel the family therapist who is provoking the emergence of too much anxiety. Outsiders who are not careful are easily run out of town. The outsider with good timing may be able to weather the storm (Lantz, 1985A) (Lantz, 1985B).

## The Primary Advantage in Marital and Family Treatment

The primary advantage in marital and family treatment is that emotional problems and psychiatric symptoms can be treated directly within the actual social context of their occurrence (Andrews, 1973) (Lantz, 1977). If dysfunctional reciprocity can be effectively challenged, the family member in pain may suddenly experience a profound level of support for the resolution of the difficulties. The family cycle of pain and despair may well suddenly change into a powerful cycle of growth and actualization. The clinical material which shortly follows (The Jones Family) illustrates the successful use of family therapy to help an adolescent female resolve an extremely uncomfortable symptom.

## The Jones Family: Extreme Itching
## Treated by a Family System Approach

Itching has been defined as a sensation or perception that produces a desire to scratch or rub the skin surface where the person feels the sensation (Musaph, 1977). According to Musaph (1977) an adequate threshold against itching sensations can be mitigated by the following factors: organic disease, at risk personality structures, a congenital or acquired disposition for a low threshold, and stress. Drugs are frequently used in the treatment of itching, although there is a general recognition that psychotherapy may become necessary if other methods fail (Gregory and Smeltzer, 1977). Psychotherapy with the itching client frequently focuses upon the individual client's tendency to repress anger and/or anxiety (Musaph, 1977) (Lantz, 1979).

At present, only little information is available in the literature pointing out the functions of itching for the total family group, or the family interaction variables important in the development of an itching family member even though a number of different family system approaches and theories (Andrews, 1974) (Minuchin, 1974) (Satir, 1967) (Zuk, 1976) would suggest that such variables and functions should exist. One purpose of this clinical material is to present a case study in which itching did serve a family function and in which family transactional patterns were important in the development of the identified patient's itching behavior. Although one case study is not statistically significant, the identification of family variables and/or the family functions of itching in one case study does have implications for family theory as well as future study in the family aspects of many dermatoses (Lantz, 1979).

## The Jones Family Referral

In January of 1977, this author was contacted by a general medical practitioner who wanted to refer a family for a family consultation interview. According to the physician, he had been treating the family's sixteen-year-old daughter for extreme itching and scratching over the last three years. The physician had tried a number of different medications, had referred the daughter to two different dermatologists, and had also referred the daughter for individual psychotherapy. None of these methods had proved successful and the physician, who had recently attended a workshop on family therapy, had the idea that the daughter's itching and scratching might be signaling a problem in the functioning of the total family group. Although it was explained to the physician that I had never worked with this type of problem previously, we agreed that I would see the family at least one time in order to determine if a family approach might be useful in this situation.

### Planning for the Interview

From a theoretical standpoint, itching and scratching in a sixteen-year-old daughter might well be a response to a family structure problem in which the daughter and one parent are over-involved, while the relationship between the father and mother is distant, double-binding activity on the part of one or both parents, or the itching response might serve the function of helping the family as a group to avoid other family behaviors such as conflict between the husband and wife. All three possibilities might lead to repressed anger and/or anxiety on the part of the daughter, which is frequently associated with the development of itching and scratching behavior.

In order to help pinpoint the family transactions that might be triggering the daughter's itching and scratching behavior, it was decided that the initial family interview would be tape recorded, and that the family session would be observed by a rater from behind a one-way mirror with the sound turned off. The rater would make an estimate of the daughter's level of itching and scratching without the benefit of sound for every three-minute interval on the level of double-bind activity occurring during the session, the level of overinvolvement between the daughter and one of the parents during the session, and the level of manifested parental conflict occurring during the 90-minute interview. The therapist met briefly with the physician and the family at the physician's office prior to the consultation interview for the purpose of providing the family with a general overview of the purpose of the consultation interview, and to obtain permission to tape the session, exchange information with the physician, and use the rater and one-way mirror. It was agreed that the daughter would continue to see the physician weekly so that he could monitor her condition and prescribe whatever medications he deemed necessary, even if we did decide on a course of family therapy.

**The Initial Sessions**

The initial session was attended by all three family members: Bob, the father, 47 years old; Beth the mother, 44 years old; and Tina, the 16 year-old daughter. During the initial part of the interview, the family therapist told the family that Tina's itching might well have an emotional component and that if this was the case, it was the therapist's opinion that an individual with such a problem generally needed help from the total family in order to solve the problem. Both parents agreed that they wanted to help. The therapist then stated that everyone could help by being as honest as possible about "all" of the problems that might be occurring within the family. The family members were instructed to "talk with each other" during the remaining part of the session about their present concerns and difficulties.

During the initial interview, it was the family therapist's subjective experience that the daughter's itching and scratching behavior increased markedly whenever the parents began to express concerns about their marital relationship. On two occasions, the parents began to intensely express resentment to each other and, at both of these times, Tina began to rub and scratch most vigorously. When Tina's scratching was noticed by the parents, they would then drop their conflict and focus on Tina and her scratching. The therapist did not experience the family as engaging in a great deal of double-binding activity, and Tina did not seem overinvolved with either parent. The family therapist's subjective opinion was confirmed after the interview when the objective rating of manifested parental conflict was compared with Tina's rate of itching and scratching. The objective data showed that an increase in Tina's scratching followed an increase in manifested parental conflict, and that a decrease in manifested parental conflict followed an increase in Tina's scratching. A decrease in scratching behavior then followed the decrease in manifested parental conflict.

After this consultation interview, the family was scheduled for a follow-up visit, at which time the family therapist was to give the family the results of the consultation and make further recommendations. It was agreed that the family physician would also attend this meeting. Tina was asked to keep a chart during the week, giving an estimate of how much itching and scratching she did everyday. She was to use the following scale: no itching, slight itching, mild itching, moderate itching, heavy itching, and extreme itching.

## Developing a Treatment Plan

In view of the conclusion that Tina's itching and scratching behavior was associated with manifested parental conflict, it was decided that the family would be given a recommendation for continued family treatment. The therapist's assessment was that the parents did have a basically stable and gratifying marital relationship, but that their efforts to negotiate and resolve conflicts were frequently interrupted by Tina's itching behavior. It was felt that Tina became overly anxious when her parents manifested conflict, and that this anxiety resulted in, and was signaled by, her itching. When the parents stopped working on their marital concerns and turned their attention towards Tina, as Tina was scratching, it reinforced Tina's experience that conflict is seldom a beneficial activity, and furthermore is seldom resolved. Tina did not obtain the experience in her daily family life that conflict could be negotiated and that it could lead to more satisfying family relationship outcomes. The cycle was reciprocal and repetitive. It resulted in a less than satisfactory marital relationship for the parents, and a continued reinforcement of Tina's anxiety and itching in response to a conflict situation.

The family therapist decided upon the following treatment plan: the family would be seen weekly for 90-minute sessions, the therapist would attempt to help the parents manifest, negotiate, and resolve marital conflict in front of Tina during the conjoint sessions, a co-therapist would be added to the treatment situation to help support Tina and help Tina handle the anxiety that she would feel in using this approach, and the sessions would all be taped and rated on the level of manifested parental conflict. A rater would monitor Tina's itching and scratching as in the first interview, Tina would be asked to continue her daily self-rating of itching behavior, the family would be told in simple words that Tina's itching and scratching did seem to be associated with manifested parental conflict, and that the therapist did not believe Tina would be able to overcome this problem until she had experienced the beneficial results of negotiated parental conflict which her itching behavior usually interrupted, and the parents would be told that they could help Tina by freely discussing their relationship difficulties in front of her, even if Tina did begin to scratch during the sessions. The family would also be told that Tina's scratching would probably increase initially. Tina would continue to see the family physician weekly so that he could monitor her condition.

It is to be noted that this counseling structure relabeled the parent's behavior when they focused upon Tina rather than continuing to work on their own marital conflict. Previously, when Tina's scratching interrupted parental conflict, the parent's behavior (focusing upon Tina) was intended to help the daughter. The counseling structure redefined this process as being less than helpful and possibly destructive. It was planned that this redefinition would interrupt the reciprocity between scratching and the decrease in manifested parental conflict.

## Assessing the Approach

The family was seen conjointly, 90-minutes each, for 16 sessions. Initially, Tina did increase her scratching as her parents began learning to manifest, negotiate, and resolve conflict issues within the marital relationship, Tina then became more comfortable, less anxious, and significantly reduced scratching and itching behavior. The family physician discontinued all of Tina's medication during the tenth week of family counseling.

As family counseling progressed, Tina continued to improve. The parents reported an improved marital relationship. By the fifteenth session, there was a significant drop in the level of manifested parental conflict. The parents reported that when they first started family counseling they tended to "save up" their problems so that they could be discussed during the family sessions. They also reported that as they became more comfortable discussing problems, they began to start "talking things out at home." They reported that many longstanding issues had been resolved and that at present both had fewer complaints and fewer resentments. By the fifteenth interview Tina was free of all acute skin damage and many of the scars were showing improvement. Tina had required no medication since the tenth week of treatment. Tina's self rating reports showed that there was an increase in the rate of itching behavior during the beginning stage of family treatment and a steady decrease as treatment continued. Family therapy was terminated by agreement with the family and the family physician at the end of the sixteenth session.

## Six-Month Follow-Up

When contacted for the six-month follow-up, all family members reported that things had continued to improve. Tina reported "no problem with itching" and Mr. and Mrs. Jones expressed happiness that the marital relationship was still improving. Mr. and Mrs. Jones reported that Tina had not had any reoccurrence of the itching problem and that all family members were in good health. The family physician reported that Tina no longer needed medical treatment for itching.

## Seven-Year Follow-Up

At the seven-year follow-up Tina was twenty-three-years-old. Her father died when Tina was nineteen from a heart attack and her mother had remarried. Tina has completed college and has started medical school. She wants to become a family practitioner. She reported that she is engaged. She vaguely remembered the problems with itching and reported that she had had no such difficulties "for years." She felt good about herself and reported a "happy life."

## Marital and Family Treatment Approaches

It has been the author's experience in a number of different treatment settings that family or marital treatment is often prescribed and utilized without a clear idea of the type of family intervention which should be used and without a clear sense of the intervention goals which the prescription or referral agent hopes to achieve. The purpose of this section of the chapter is to briefly describe eight different forms of family intervention, realistic goals for each intervention form and the differential use of each family treatment form. It is hoped that this model will be useful to clinical practitioners and that the model will help bring additional clarity in comprehensive treatment planning. It should be noted that this model is based upon the author's subjective experience and that the model has not been subjected to systematic research.

## Eight Family Intervention Forms

The eight approaches to family intervention which will be described are the supportive-informational approach, the crisis intervention approach, the psychoeducational approach, the supportive-problem solving approach, the interactional approach, the psychoanalytic approach, the existential approach, and the crisis induction approach. Although all eight different approaches share a few common concepts such as the idea that the family is a system of interlocking and reciprocal human relationships, the eight approaches are quite different in their goals, value assumptions and operational technologies (Lantz and Thorward, 1985).

## The Supportive-Informational Approach

The supportive-informational approach should be used initially whenever a client is admitted as an inpatient into a psychiatric hospital. The primary goals of this approach include helping the client's family develop a positive alliance with the psychiatric hospital or agency, helping the family decrease anxiety about the hospitalization process and helping the family exchange information about the client, the hospital, and the family background with the hospital or agency treatment team. Such goals assume that the client's family will be anxious during the first part of the hospitalization process and that the structure of the hospital milieu and culture will be confusing for the family (Stewart, 1981). Such goals also assume that the family will need support and clarification in order for the family to make a strong commitment to the hospital treatment program. Family intervention techniques utilized in the supportive-information approach include acceptance, support, clarification, guilt reduction activities, responsible information sharing, structure and the provision of experiences that socialize the family about the hospital's philosophy of treatment as well as the bureaucratic procedures inherent in the hospitalization process (Stewart, 1981).

After the family has developed at least a partial alliance with the hospital, a decision can be made to change the type of family intervention used with the client and the family. Such a decision should be based upon a good assessment of both the client, and the family system and the hospital or agency treatment team should be able to articulate clear reasons for any change. Any family intervention change can potentially damage the hospital family alliance and should not be risked unless the potential benefits of such a change out weigh the possible dangers (Lantz and Thorward, 1985).

## The Crisis Intervention Approach

The crisis intervention approach is used when the client and/or the family are experiencing a true crisis. A true crisis occurs when a situational or developmental event interferes with the client or the family's ability to use previously effective coping and problem solving skills (Lantz, 1978) (Dixon, 1979). A true crisis is often signaled by the rapid onset of anxiety or depression which is reactive to a specific triggering event and which also follows a long period of adequate social functioning. In the crisis intervention approach the family therapist and the family join together in an effort to identify the triggering event, discuss how the triggering event has disrupted individual and family functioning patterns and to discover alternative methods of coping which will resolve the crisis (Aguilera and Messick, 1978). In this approach, the family therapist specifically attempts to help the family discover alternative environmental support systems which could help restore equilibrium, alternative family interactional patterns and alternative coping skills that each family member can use to resolve the crisis (Aguilera and Messick, 1978) (Dixon, 1979).

Family crisis intervention is most often utilized in emergency psychiatric settings and short-term inpatient psychiatric units. Family crisis intervention is only appropriately used in a true crisis situation. Diagnostic categories which most frequently fit into the model of a true crisis situation include developmental and situational adjustment disorders, situational forms of marital and family conflict and various occupational and social adjustment problems triggered by environmental and economic change. Crisis intervention is most often inappropriately utilized when the clinical practitioner fails to take a good history and confuses a long-term pattern of chaotic functioning with a true crisis situation (Lantz and Thorward, 1985).

## The Psychoeducational Approach

The psychoeducational approach to family intervention is primarily utilized with families that include at least one schizophrenic family member whose illness is considered to have a major biological component.

Psychoeducational family therapy is based upon the idea that the schizophrenic family member has a core psychological and/or biochemical deficit which makes the client particularly vulnerable to high expressed emotionality in his or her family environment (Anderson, Hogarty and Reiss, 1980). This model assumes that when the patient is subjected to such expressed emotionality there is an increased risk for client deterioration and increased psychotic behavior. The schizophrenic client's family often experiences a sense of guilt, anger and/or frustration which is reactive to the client's symptoms and problems. This family emotionality is then communicated to the schizophrenic family member who in turn reacts by again increasing the manifestation of psychotic symptoms. An ongoing vicious circle is the result (Anderson, Hogarty and Reiss, 1980) (Lantz, 1982A) (Lantz, 1985B) (Lantz, 1985A).

In the psychoeducational approach the primary intervention goal is to decrease high expressed emotionality in the client's family group. This is done by helping the family reduce their feelings of guilt, by teaching the family about some of the biological components of schizophrenia, by helping the family discover and join support groups where feelings can be safely discussed and discharged and by teaching the family about the concept of high expressed emotionality so that the family members can more easily take a kind, but matter of fact attitude towards the schizophrenic client. The initial research on this intervention form suggests that the psychoeducational appraoch does have value in decreasing the occurrence of rehospitalization and in lengthening the time periods between hospitalization (Anderson, Hogerty and Reiss, 1980) (Lantz, 1986C).

## The Supportive-Problem Solving Approach

The supportive-problem solving approach is utilized with family groups in which the family members have chronic difficulties in problem solving and/or ego functioning (Perlman, 1979). Such families are usually described as including family members with neurotic and/or personality disorder difficulties. At times, this approach can be combined with other modalities in the treatment of psychotic clients. The major goal in the supportive-problem solving approach is to exercise and support each family member's ego. This is done by teaching the family members problem solving skills and by helping the family achieve realistic goals and realistic family daily living tasks (Perlman, 1979).

In the supportive-problem solving approach, the family therapist provides the family with both limit setting and structure, offers the family a combination of encouragement and support, and lets the family borrow the therapist's ego in the family's problem solving activities. The supportive-problem solving approach has traditionally been used in family service agencies, but can also be quite appropriately utilized in a psychiatric setting. The author has found this approach to be very useful with manic-depressive clients when the approach is combined with individual therapy and pharmacotherapy (Lantz and Thorward, 1985).

## The Interactional Approach

The interactional approach is most often used when an individual's primary symptom cluster seems to have a family communication function. In the interactional approach, the therapist views the development of symptoms within an individual family member as being a signal which indicates that the total family group is having difficulty in family communication (Satir, 1967). Interactional family therapy assumes that the therapist's primary function is to stimulate and teach the family as a group to communicate in a more functional way and that such an improvement in family communication will trigger a reduction in the manifestation of family and individual symptoms (Andrews, 1973). Although the literature suggests that this approach can be utilized across the diagnostic spectrum (Satir, 1967) it has been this author's experience that the interactional approach is most useful with clients exhibiting neurotic, adjustment reaction, and personality disorder problems. The author also has found the interactional approach to be particularly useful in psychosomatic and psychophysiological disorders (Lantz, 1979).

In the interactional approach, the family therapist uses modeling, confrontation, support, interactional guidance and clarification to help family members send each other messages in a clear, precise and congruent way. The family therapist also uses clarification, reframing, relabeling and interpretation to help all family members more accurately decode and evaluate the messages they receive from other family members. Homework assignments, therapeutic directives and supportive statements from the therapist are also used to reinforce the authority of the parental dyad. This is done because interactional family therapists believe that parents are the leaders of the family and that parental authority is extremely useful and helpful in preventing the occurrence and/or continuation of dysfunctional family communication within the primary family group (Lantz, 1977) (Lantz, 1978A) (Andrews, 1979) (Lantz and Thorward, 1985).

## The Psychoanalytic Approach

Psychoanalytic principles and concepts are frequently used with modification in the crisis intervention, problem solving and interactional approaches to family therapy intervention. True psychoanalytic family therapy is called family psychoanalysis and has only rarely been used as a primary intervention form (Grotjahn, 1960).

Family psychoanalysis requires extensive training in both psychoanalysis and in family therapy. Few mental health practitioners have the background required to successfully combine the two modalities. A brief review of the literature suggests that family psychoanalysis is used only when all individual family members are appropriate candidates for individual psychoanalysis, and only when it is determined that the reciprocal nature of the interactional patterns within the family will tend to facilitate the analytic process (Grotjahn, 1960). It is the author's understanding that family psychoanalysis is used most frequently with families that include members with neurotic difficulties. Again, it is helpful to remember that psychoanalytic concepts are extremely helpful in the understanding of the family group and that these concepts can be appropriately used with modifications in techniques when combined with the crisis intervention, supportive-problem solving and interactional approaches to family therapy intervention (Lantz and Thorward, 1985).

## The Existential Approach

Existential family therapy is a highly confrontive form of conjoint family therapy intervention which is based upon the existential concepts of responsible action, meaning and bad faith (Lantz, 1982A) (Lantz, 1986C). In existential family therapy, it is assumed that when family members fail to responsibly act in ways that stimulate the discovery, recognition and awareness of meaning in the family's daily existence, that the family members will experience feelings of bad faith (Andrews, 1979). Feelings of bad faith have been described as a sense of emptiness, dullness, and the feeling that something is missing in life (Andrews, 1979). This feeling of bad faith has also been described as a feeling of anomie (Andrews, 1979). In many instances, family members cover and suppress the experience of bad faith through the consumption of toxic substances such as alcohol and drugs (Lantz and Thorward, 1985) (Lantz, 1986C).

In existential family therapy, the family therapist attempts to stimulate all family members to take responsible action in an effort to discover existential meaning in shared family living experiences. Such meanings can be found through new attitudinal stances that family members develop towards each other, through productive contributions that family members make for each other and through the experience of shared intimacy and acceptance between family members (Lantz, 1986C). Treatment techniques utilized in existential family therapy include the confrontive and open expression by the therapist of the therapist's subjective experience of being with the family group, provocative interpretations and clarifications about each instance of family bad faith demonstrated by the family members during the time and space of the conjoint family therapy interview and the therapist's skill in highlighting to the family members that they are wasting precious moments of existence by failing to recognize their importance to each other during the present moment in time (Andrews, 1979) (Lantz, 1985A).

Existential family therapy is most appropriately used if family members are experiencing feelings of anomie and/or bad faith when these feelings are not the result of an affective disorder, thought disorder or neurotic process. Existential family therapy can be used effectively with many personality disorder clients and with some clients who have chemical dependency problems. Existential family therapy should not be used with clients who have major ego deficits as the process is extremely confrontive and may stimulate too much anxiety for such clients (Lantz and Thorward, 1985) (Lantz, 1986C).

## The Crisis Induction Approach

The central idea in the crisis induction approach is that most human problems are systematically reinforced by the family context in which they occur. Crisis induction therapists believe that an effective and powerful strategy to use in such a situation is to strategically induce a family crisis which will interrupt the family's ability to reinforce the problem behavior (Lantz and Thorward, 1985).

In this author's opinion, the crisis induction approach should only be used with great care and only when other methods of intervention have failed. The crisis induction approach is useful because it creates anxiety in the family system which in turn produces motivation for change. Since the approach does generate increased family anxiety it should be considered dangerous with some families. The crisis induction approach seems to be most appropriately used in an inpatient psychiatric setting with families who have not been able to utilize any other treatment approach and who have a member who chronically returns to the psychiatric hospital because the family sabotages the aftercare plan. The approach also calls for a high degree of skill and judgment on the part of the therapist and should not be used by the beginning practitioner (Lantz and Thorward, 1985).

Family therapy can be an important and useful treatment modality. Clear and specific goals for family therapy intervention and a realistic understanding of what can be accomplished by the different family therapy approaches can be extremely useful to clinical practitioners in both treatment planning and treatment implementation. The inappropriate use of any family intervention form can increase the risk of damaging the client.

## Summary

A treatment modality is like a treatment technique in the sense that neither can directly help a client. The modality is only useful if it is respectfully implemented by the therapist in a way that stimulates the emergence of one or more curative factors. Different modalities provide the client with different opportunities for growth. The therapist has a responsibility to try and carefully select the modality that will provide each client with the maximum possibility for help.

## Chapter Four

# TREATMENT STAGES

The basic and primary goal in clinical social work is to help the client develop additional balance and flexibility in the client's social functioning patterns. Since many factors contribute to the occurrence of dysfunctional patterns it often becomes necessary for the social worker to use many different treatment techniques and modalities to help the client achieve the primary treatment goal (Lantz, 1978A).

Intervention can be directed towards the biological, psychological, family and/or towards the social contextual aspects of social functioning. Such a variety of appropriate intervention methods may result in a chaotic treatment process. The broadly eclectic use of many different intervention methods during psychosocial treatment demands a method of providing a degree of structure during the process of treatment. The utilization of a treatment stage format is useful in providing such structure. The described treatment approach includes the joining stage, the assessment stage, the prescription recommendation stage, the implementation stage, the enhancement stage, the termination stage, the deterioration stage, the resistance stage, the clarification stage, and the insight stage (Lantz, 1986B). These ten stages of treatment are illustrated in Figure Number Four.

The ten stages should be considered as treatment steps organized into a therapeutic cycle. The various steps blend into each other and do not have rigid boundaries. At times the total cycle is repeated and repeated numerous times during the client's treatment program. At other times clients will go through the treatment cycle rapidly and some clients will even be able to skip part of the cycle. The client's progress through the treatment cycle is directed by the client's need rather than the therapist's theoretical expectations. For example, some clients are able to change social functioning patterns without developing insight into the reasons for the use of older dysfunctional patterns (Lantz, 1986B) (Rabkin, 1983). Other clients are not able to change dysfunctional patterns without the occurrence of extensive insight into the developmental reasons for these patterns (Hollis, 1972) (Lantz, 1986B). The ten stage cycle

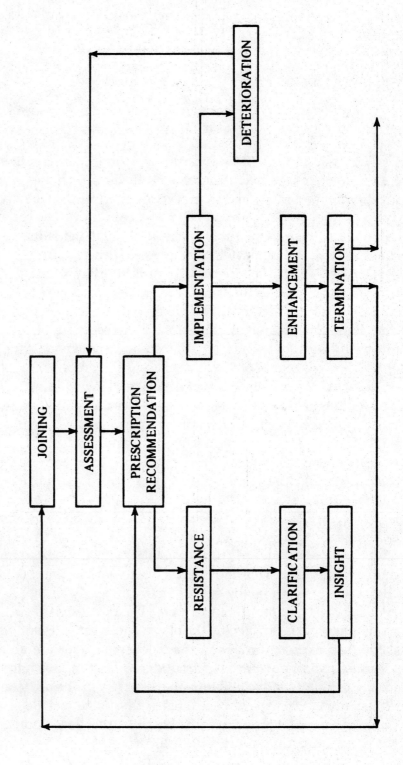

Figure 4

STAGES IN CLINICAL SOCIAL WORK PRACTICE

model is able to accommodate both kinds of client systems (Lantz, 1986B).

### The Joining Stage

The joining stage is the initial stage in all forms of casework, counseling and psychotherapy. In the joining stage the therapist and client system make contact with each other for the first time and begin to develop a professional treatment relationship. In this stage the worker and client start to know each other and begin to decide upon the goals and perimeters of treatment.

In the joining stage the client will manifest his or her primary social functioning pattern to the therapist as the client and therapist begin to develop their relationship. For example, the client who uses an attacking pattern will tend to attack the therapist, the client who uses an avoiding pattern will tend to avoid the therapist, and the client who uses a dependency pattern will try to lean on the therapist to meet all or most of the client's dependency needs.

The joining stage of treatment is an anxiety stimulating situation for the client. In many instances the client has never previously been in treatment. Even if the client has had a previous treatment experience, this experience has often been with a different therapist, or the experience has occurred for a different set of reasons. The joining stage represents a new situation for the client, and as a result the client will attempt to utilize his or her primary social functioning pattern in an attempt to control the process of this new situation so that anxiety will be minimized (Lantz, 1986B).

The therapist's major task during the joining stage is to set up a treatment atmosphere which will allow the client to engage in treatment, and at the same time will not allow the client to totally control the treatment process through the use of the client's primary social functioning pattern (Lantz, 1986B). For example, when a dependency pattern client begins treatment, the client will demand that the therapist be a person who will let the client "lean" and who will meet most of the client's dependency needs. If the therapist refuses to meet any of the client's dependency needs the client will generally drop out of treatment. The dependency form of social functioning has been the client's major strategy for meeting needs, and if the therapist does not let the client manifest this style to some degree the client will feel defenseless. On the other hand, if the therapist makes a covert arrangement with the client to be a person who will meet all of the client's dependency needs, the client will end up controlling treatment and the therapist will be totally reinforcing the client's dysfunctional social functioning pattern. Treatment will eventually fail as the client is not encouraged to change (Lantz, 1986A) (Lantz, 1986B).

A good general rule for the therapist in the joining stage of treatment is to try and maintain a balanced interactional pattern with the client yet at the same time the therapist should lean towards accepting or mirroring the client's major pattern to some extent. Such acceptance or mirroring should occur at a level that is less than what the client desires, but which is high enough to allow the client some relief from anxiety. The therapist should be accepting of the client's pattern, yet at the same time the therapist should try not to totally reinforce the client's pattern. This attitude on the part of the therapist will provide the client with some support, yet at the same time it will also provide some confrontation. Effective treatment always includes a balance of both support and confrontation (Andrews, 1972) (Lantz, 1980) (Lantz, 1986B).

It is unfortunate to note that much of the professional literature written about the joining stage or relationship building stage of treatment is off the mark, because it fails to point out that different clients need different kinds of acceptance and attention during the joining stage. Joining methods and techniques such as warmth, empathy, caring and unconditional positive regard are generally considered to be both safe and effective tools during the joining stage (Rogers, 1961). Unfortunately this is sometimes incorrect. The fact is that too much warmth, empathy, caring, or unconditional positive regard initially can be dangerous, and can result in a premature termination of treatment with both the avoiding pattern client and the attacking pattern client. Warmth, empathy, caring and unconditional positive regard work very well with a dependency pattern client, but these techniques often stimulate too much anxiety with the attacking and avoiding types of clients, especially during the joining stage (Lantz, 1985A).

The avoiding pattern client uses avoidance to escape anxiety and human contact. Human contact is considered dangerous by such clients, and the therapist who attempts to be too warm, or too caring, will often push such clients away. The avoiding type of client is more likely to engage in treatment if the therapist uses a matter-of-fact joining approach and does not try to use excessive warmth to "capture" the client.

The attacking pattern client is seldom able to respect the therapist who is too "warm" during the joining stage. Such clients believe that it is important to "attack first" and such clients will simply distrust any therapist who cannot use, or be comfortable with, some hostility and aggression. Although it is important for the therapist to avoid matching the client's level of hostility, it is also equally important that the therapist demonstrate quickly that the therapist can set limits, that the therapist has a degree of comfort with angry feelings, and that the therapist can use assertive behavior (Lantz and Thorward, 1985).

One method of identifying countertransference, especially during the joining stage of treatment, is to examine to what degree the therapist abandons the balanced interactional pattern with the client. Whenever the therapist uses a rigid and/or extreme form of any communication pattern with the client, the therapist could be considered to be manifesting countertransference and countertransference feelings. In such instances the therapist is not using controlled emotional involvement (Lantz, 1985B).

### Controlled Emotional Involvement

The concept of controlled emotional involvement is extremely important during joining. Controlled emotional involvement can be defined as the therapist's conscious use of his or her own feelings during the treatment process to help the client have a successful treatment experience (Hollis, 1972). A major part of this definition revolves around the idea of the conscious use of the therapist's feelings to help the client meet the client's treatment needs. Controlled emotional involvement should not be directed towards the meeting of just the therapist's needs. The following case illustration demonstrates a therapist's use of anxiety and avoidance to meet the therapist's needs while working with an aggressive client. The case illustration will then be continued to demonstrate how a different worker was able to consciously use assertive behavior and appropriate aggression to help the same client join in treatment.

### The Saunders Case

Mr. Saunders was referred to a mental health center by his probation officer. Mr. Saunders had a long history of aggressive behavior. He had been arrested on a number of different occasions for assult. He had been divorced by his wife because he beat her, and he had lost many jobs due to his overly aggressive style of social functioning. Mr. Saunders did not want to be in treatment but was forced into the treatment situation by his probation officer who made treatment a part of Mr. Saunders's probation program.

Mr. Saunders was very threatening to his therapist during his initial visit to the mental health center. Mr. Saunders told his therapist that he would hurt her if she gave his probation officer a bad report. He also told the therapist that she had better not ask him any personal questions during the interview as, "I lose my temper real easy." Although the therapist was able to make it through the interview she somehow managed to schedule Mr. Saunders's second appointment for the following month rather than in a week which was her general routine with new clients. The therapist happened to be sick on the day of Mr. Saunders's second appointment.

After the therapist was finally able to talk over her feelings about Mr. Saunders with her supervisor, Mr. Saunders was transferred to a new therapist. The transfer occurred because the supervisor did not believe that the first therapist would be able to overcome her "moving away" pattern rapidly enough to help Mr. Saunders join in treatment. The second therapist was an alcoholism counselor with considerable experience with aggressive clients. She was comfortable with limit setting. She called Mr. Saunders to set up his second appointment.

In Mr. Saunders's second interview his new therapist told him openly that he had been given a new therapist because he had threatened and scared the first therapist. The new therapist told Mr. Saunders that she would be giving his probation officer monthly reports and that any threatening behavior on his part in the future would result in the therapist terminating Mr. Saunders from treatment. She stated that she imagined that the probation officer would consider this to be a probation violation. The second therapist also told Mr. Saunders that she would feel free to ask any questions she wanted to ask. She stated that she believed that Mr. Saunders had every right to refuse to answer any questions that he felt were inappropriate, but that any loss of temper that looked threatening would be reported to his probation officer. Mr. Saunders made no further threatening gestures to the new therapist and was eventually able to benefit from therapy. The therapist's ability to set limits and to be comfortable with angry feelings made it possible for Mr. Saunders to join in treatment. Mr. Saunders told the new therapist that he liked her because, "You don't take any crap from people."

### Treatment Teaching During the Joining Stage

Treatment teaching refers to the process of defining and specifying for the client the perimeters of the treatment process and the treatment relationship (Osipow, Walsh, and Tosi, 1980). During the joining stage it is important for the therapist to help the client develop realistic expectations about the treatment process and also to teach the client about the procedures and perimeters which are a part of treatment. Teaching the client about these procedures and treatment perimeters gives the client some basic knowledge about how to have a successful treatment experience. Such perimeters can be related to the length and frequency of treatment appointments, the relationship and activities that occur between the client and the therapist, the cost of treatment, or about the role of both the therapist and the client (Osipow, Walsh, and Tosi, 1980).

Such treatment perimeters can be structured too rigidly, or can be made so that they are too flexible (Rabkin, 1983). If the therapist is overly rigid in defining the perimeters of treatment the client will often feel frustrated, restricted and resistive. The client may terminate treatment because the client perceives the therapist as too demanding and the treatment process as too difficult (Osipow, Walsh, and Tosi, 1980). A second difficulty which can occur if the therapist is too rigid about the perimeters of treatment is that the therapist may inhibit his or her own flexibility during the treatment process. Since treatment is always a two person process it is important for the therapist to remember that any treatment rule that is made must be followed by both the therapist and the client. Whenever the therapist becomes overly rigid about the perimeters of treatment in an attempt to control the client, the therapist is also setting up a situation where the therapist is controlling his or her own flexibility and creativity.

A third difficulty which can result from overly rigid treatment perimeters is that by overstructuring the treatment process the therapist often sets up a situation which reinforces the client's dependency needs. This occurs because the therapist has assumed too much control. This then can minimize the client's opportunity to practice independence (Osipow, Walsh, and Tosi, 1980). Another problem is that when the therapist takes too much control, the client is often stimulated to use intellectualization defenses when talking about feelings and problems. The client may feel restricted, and the use of intellectualization may seem to be a safer approach.

An additional difficulty which can result from the overly rigid definition of treatment perimeters is that by taking too much control the therapist may give the client the idea that if the client just follows the treatment program that things will "always get better." The client may develop false hopes for success reactive to the therapist's structure. If, and when, the client does not experience wonderful results the client may internalize the blame and become depressed. Psychosocial treatment is always a two person process and responsibility for the process should be shared as much as is realistically possible (Andrews, 1979) (Lantz, 1985B).

At times the perimeters of treatment can be defined in a way that is too flexible. In such situations the client may experience excessive confusion reactive to a lack of structure (Osipow, Walsh, and Tosi, 1980). Such confusion can also stimulate or reinforce client dependency feelings. If the client experiences feelings of anxiety about the start of treatment, a lack of structure about the perimeters of treatment may stimulate the client to see the therapist as an all powerful figure whose "every word" should be listened to as if it was the "word of God."

The client is usually anxious at the start of treatment and often has little knowledge about effective styles of work during treatment. The therapist's failure to provide any structure may result in the client's inability to focus on problem solving in a useful way. The client may talk about irrelevant aspects of problem areas, and the client may not be able to develop a meaningful system for understanding personal behavior (Osipow, Walsh, and Tosi, 1980). The client may decide to terminate treatment because the client fails to learn how the process of treatment can be helpful (Lantz, 1978A). An effective general rule for the therapist is to attempt to be flexible about the less important treatment, and inflexible about the important rules, such as the rules against allowing the client to use the therapist as only a friend, or as something other than a professional helper. As Whittaker and Malone (1953) have noted, the therapist must be both tender and tough when helping the client learn to use treatment in a realistic way.

## Characteristics of the Effective Psychotherapist

Three important characteristics of the effective psychotherapist have already been noted. The first characteristic is the therapist's ability to use and manifest a balanced social functioning pattern with the client during the treatment process. The second important characteristic of the therapist is the ability to use controlled emotional involvement in a way that helps the client meet the client's treatment needs. The third characteristic is the therapist's ability to use both structure and flexibility to help the client join in treatment. Additional characteristics of the effective therapist include the ability to manifest empathy, acceptance, openness, and confrontation. All of these characteristics are particularly important during joining (Lantz, 1986B).

## Empathy

Rogers (1961) defines empathy as the therapist's ability to understand the feelings and thoughts of the client in a way that is accurately communicated to the client. Empathy is a process of communicating the therapist's inferences about the underlying meaning of the client's words, back to the client in a way that helps the client feel that he or she is being understood. Understanding on the part of the therapist is generally not much help unless the client perceives that the therapist understands. Empathy does not necessarily mean agreement. In many instances the client will feel considerable relief after the client discovers that the therapist is willing to work hard to understand the client's thoughts and feelings, even if the therapist disagrees with the client's perceptions about the self or the world at large (Perlman, 1979) (Mosak, 1979).

## Acceptance

Acceptance can be defined as the therapist's willingness to suspend judgmental evaluations about the client as a person, even if the therapist personally disagrees with the client's ideas, values, and style of social living (Lantz, 1978A). Acceptance does not mean the reinforcement of the client's values, ideas and behavior. It implies an acknowledgement by the therapist that self-defeating behavior on the part of the client can be understood, and that a person is of value even if the person exhibits such self-defeating behavior (Osipow, Walsh, and Tosi, 1980). Again, acceptance is not much help unless the client perceives that he or she is being accepted as a person by the therapist (Osipow, Walsh, and Tosi, 1980).

## Openness

Openness can be defined as a willingness on the part of the therapist to be a person with the client (Andrews, 1979). Although it is absolutely important that the therapist use his or her time with the client to help the client meet the client's treatment needs, this can be done in a way that reveals the therapist to be a living person as opposed to a technological helping machine. The myth of the therapist is as a blank screen has even been replaced in psychoanalytic circles with the concept of the therapist as a person who can use many varieties of both action and silence to communicate warmth, empathy and encouragement (Sherman, 1983) (Gedo, 1979).

## Confrontation

Confrontation can be defined as the process of helping the client review and/or modify thoughts, feelings or behavior. Confrontation occurs whenever the therapist attempts to stimulate the client to use a new or different perceptual set in the client's evaluation of the self, the world, or the client's functioning in the world. Treatment cannot effectively occur unless some confrontation is included in the process. Confrontation about client problems is much more helpful to the client than is the provision of indiscriminate, naive and pseudo-accepting "therapeutic" responses (Osipow, Walsh, and Tosi, 1980). Kind and firm confrontations by the therapist can stimulate the client to see the therapist as competent, caring, professional, concerned and trustworthy (Andrews, 1972) (Corlis and Rabe, 1969) (Mosak, 1979).

## The Assessment Stage

The second stage is the assessment stage. This stage begins before joining is completed and can often be helpful to the therapist and the client in their efforts to join with each other in a treatment relationship. The primary treatment goals during the assessment stage are for the therapist and client to discover the major problematic social functioning patterns that the client is using in his or her present psychosocial situation, to discover the major problematic patterns that the client has used throughout the client's life and to begin to discover some of the influencing factors which have stimulated the occurrence of these problematic patterns.

Assessment should occur (at least partially) before the occurrence of intervention. Assessment provides the client and therapist with some good ideas about the direction that treatment should follow and about intervention approaches which could be useful. Assessment techniques which are frequently utilized in the assessment stage include person-situation reflection, interactional pattern reflection, influencing factor reflection, the mental status exam, psychological testing, the taking of a social history, discussing dreams and early recollections, observing the client's functioning within the interview situation, collecting information from significant others, projective drawings, the physical examination, the neurological examination, taking a health history, and the therapist's examination of his or her own feelings that occur in response to the client and to the client's psychosocial situation (Lantz, 1978A) (Basch, 1980) (Alexander, 1950).

The clinical social worker uses many of the familiar assessment tools utilized by other helping professionals but, uses these techniques and tools in a slightly different manner. During the assessment stage the clinical social worker utilizes every assessment tool to help answer four questions. The four questions are: "What is the client's primary social functioning pattern?," "How has this pattern created difficulty for the client?" "What influencing factors have significantly stimulated the development of the client's primary pattern?" and "What methods can be used to stimulate additional flexibility and balance for the client in the client's life?" This assessment attitude can be elaborated upon by discussing one specific technique; the social study in greater detail.

## The Social Study

The social study can be a good way to help the client begin to reveal information about personal difficulties and social functioning problems to the therapist in a way that does not need to generate overwhelming anxiety. Asking the client about his or her past history can often help the client talk about the self in a way that partially removes the client from the client's present encounter with both the self and with the therapist (Corlis and Rabe, 1969). The client will frequently feel more comfortable talking about the past than about present feelings, problems and social functioning patterns.

The information that the client reveals during the taking of the social history can be utilized in two distinct ways. First, the information can be utilized in an explanatory way by accepting the information as an initial view of the nodal events of the client's life which were important influencing factors in the client's development. Although this explanatory use of social history information can provide the therapist with good clues about how the client may have evolved into his or her present situation, the explanatory approach does not necessarily tell the therapist much about the client's present situation or functioning patterns. The explanatory use of social history information is not exclusively utilized by most clinical social workers (Lantz, 1978A).

A second way to utilize social history information is to use it as a social functioning descriptive tool (Mosak, 1979). In the descriptive approach it is assumed that the client's memory of past events is distorted in a direction towards the client's present social functioning patterns. In other words, it is assumed that the client's memory of past events will describe more about the person's present social functioning patterns, than it will describe about what really happened in the past (Corlis and Rabe, 1969). In the descriptive approach the client's memory of the past is utilized as a word drawing that can be interpreted to give the social worker information about the client's present social living patterns (Mosak, 1979). For example, a client's memory of "I was alone a lot when I was young" might be interpreted descriptively to mean "I am presently a person who spends a lot of time alone," "I am a loner," or "I feel most comfortable when I move away from other people." The descriptive use of social history information is favored by many clinical social workers because it seems to more effectively provide the therapist with information about the client's primary style of social functioning. Many clinical social workers favor the descriptive use of most assessment tools. At the same time, the effective social worker is always willing to accept the explanatory use of any assessment tool when this is helpful (Lantz, 1978A).

Towards the end of the assessment stage, the therapist and the client should have a fairly good idea of both the primary social functioning patterns that the client uses to solve emotional and social problems, a beginning idea of those influencing factors which have stimulated the development of such patterns, and a few ideas about how the therapist can help the client increase flexibility and balance within the client's primary social functioning pattern. At this point the client and the therapist move into the prescription recommendation stage (Lantz, 1986B).

### The Prescription Recommendation Stage

During the prescription recommendation stage the therapist offers the client a social living recommendation. Such a recommendation is designed to stimulate the development of increased flexibility and balance within the client's primary social functioning pattern. The recommendation can be directed towards medical, psychological, or environmental aspects of the client's social functioning pattern. For example, a client who uses a "moving away from others" pattern can be asked to join a psychotherapy group in order to help the client challenge the client's pattern of social isolation. The same client can be asked to take antianxiety medication to help the client control the anxiety which helps the client move away from people and problems, and the client can also be asked to join a community social club in order to help the client develop the situational opportunities which are necessary in order for the client to make new friends and expand his or her social network (Lantz, 1986B).

Prescription recommendations can also be broken down into two categories. The categories are internal recommendations and external recommendations. Internal recommendations are designed to help the client change personal patterns and problems, and external recommendations are designed to help change the client's social environment in a way that promotes, encourages and maximizes the client's opportunity to make internal changes. An external recommendation is generally accompanied by, or connected with, an internal recommendation. Again, such prescription recommendations can be directed towards the modification of medical, psychological, and social environment problems (Lantz, 1986B).

### Medical Prescription Recommendations

Medications and other medical treatments can often be extremely helpful to the client who is trying to modify a social functioning pattern. Such treatment should always be prescribed by a medical doctor. The non-medical practitioner should develop and maintain an open and close working relationship with an appropriately trained physician when working with clients who might benefit from medical interventions.

Medications can be helpful to the client because such medications can help control or decrease feeling states which facilitate and/or stimulate the client's use of a particular social functioning pattern (Lieb and Slaby, 1975). For example, a dependency pattern client who experiences strong feelings of depression can often be helped by the prescription of an antidepressant medication. The connection between depression and a rigid dependency pattern is reciprocal in that the feeling of depression often facilitates the use of a dependency pattern (Rado, 1958B). At the same time, the use of inflexible dependency patterns stimulate the occurrence of the feeling state of depression (Rado, 1958A). Providing the client with an antidepressant medication can help the client experience some relief from his or her feelings of depression, and can also provide the client with a better opportunity to modify the dependency movement pattern because this pattern is now being facilitated to a lesser degree by the feelings of depression (Lieb and Slaby, 1975).

Numerous psychotropic medications have been developed which can help the client control or minimize feelings of anxiety, depression, and chronic states of anger or rage. Since each of these feelings has an interactional facilitation component (Rado, 1958A) medications should then be considered to be an intervention approach which at times can help the client modify social movement patterns (Lieb and Slaby, 1975).

## Psychological Prescription Recommendations

A psychological recommendation can be defined as any activity recommended by the therapist and implemented by the client which is designed to help the client change thoughts, beliefs or feeling states which help the client maintain a dysfunctional social functioning pattern. Examples of such recommendations include relaxation training activities, imagery experiences, cognitive restructuring exercises, and client controlled behavior modification activities (Osipow, Walsh, and Tosi, 1980).

## Social Prescription Recommendations

A social recommendation can be defined as any activity recommended by the therapist and implemented by the client which is designed to help the client modify social components of the client's social functioning pattern (Lantz, 1986B). For example, a shy, withdrawn and meek client who uses a moving away from people and problems pattern can be asked to "Act as if you are John Wayne for one week." Such a recommendation can give the client a specific approach towards experimenting with social change. The following case illustrates the use of social prescription recommendations.

Mr. Hall is a 37 year-old single male who has suffered with recurrent episodes of depression for the past twenty years. He lives with his elderly parents and has never been able to establish consistent employment or independent living. Although Mr. Hall's psychiatrist believes that there is a large biochemical component as a part of Mr. Hall's recurrent depressions, the psychiatrist also believes that Mr. Hall's parents overprotect Mr. Hall and help keep him dependent through their constant efforts to be of help. The psychiatrist also believes that Mr. Hall uses and leans on his parents pathologically and that "staying at home all day" reinforces Mr. Hall's depressions. Mr. Hall's psychiatrist arranged for Mr. Hall to attend a psychiatric day treatment hospital five days a week. Mr. Hall returned home at night from the day treatment facility. The staff at the day treatment hospital encouraged Mr. Hall to learn independent social problem solving skills. The staff felt comfortable letting Mr. Hall struggle with problems and refused to help unless Mr. Hall had first "given it a real strong effort." After a six month period of time Mr. Hall gained confidence in his own ability to solve problems. Mr. Hall was eventually able to get and keep a job.

One of two client responses generally occurs after the social worker provides the client with a prescription recommendation. One response is to implement the recommendation. If this occurs the client and the therapist move into the implementation stage (see figure number four). The second possible response is to resist the recommendation. If this occurs the therapist and client move into the resistance stage of treatment. (See figure number four.)

## The Implementation Stage

In the implementation stage of treatment the client makes an honest and consistent effort to implement the therapist's recommendation. In this stage the client is open to change and does not manifest significant resistance. At times the client is able to rapidly implement the recommendation with little effort. This occurs primarily when the client is unable to solve his or her presenting problem due to a lack of information and knowledge, or when the recommendation is not too complex. At other times, the implementation stage takes a longer period of time. This occurs when the recommendation to be implemented is more complex and/or when the implementation of the recommendation needs to include practice and repetition (Lantz, 1986). Again, significant resistance is not a part of the implementation stage (Lantz, 1986B).

Two client responses can occur reactive to the implementation stage. One response is called deterioration and the other response is called enhancement (see figure number four).

### The Enhancement Stage

The enhancement stage of clinical social work follows the implementation stage. The enhancement stage is the result of the client's implementation of the therapist's recommendation. This stage only occurs when the client makes an honest and consistent effort to implement the recommendation and when the recommendation is based upon a good assessment and is effectively designed to help the client increase flexibility in his or her problem solving skills (Lantz, 1986B) (Andrews, 1972).

During the enhancement stage the client experiences considerable relief from uncomfortable emotions and also experiences the benefit of increased flexibility and balance in his or her social functioning pattern. The enhancement stage precedes the termination stage. (See figure number four.)

### The Termination Stage

The termination stage of treatment follows the enhancement stage. In termination the client and the therapist agree that the client has achieved the client's treatment goals. The client feels better, evidences increased flexibility and balance within his or her social functioning pattern and the client is also able to generalize what the client has learned to other social living situations and to possible future problems. The therapist and the client celebrate the client's efforts and success during the termination stage (Corlis and Rabe, 1969) (Lantz, 1986B).

At times the termination stage represents the last contact between the client and the social worker. At other times the client will come back to see the social worker at a later point in time when a new problem occurs. At other times the client will request that the social worker help the client solve a secondary set of problems which have come to the forefront of the client's awareness after the client has had an initially successful treatment experience. When this occurs the social worker and the client complete the termination stage through celebration and then start again to develop a totally new treatment contract by moving back to the joining stage (Lantz, 1986B). (See figure number four.)

## The Deterioration Stage

Like enhancement, the deterioration stage of treatment also follows the implementation stage. This stage occurs whenever the client makes an honest, effective and consistent effort to implement the therapist's recommendation and then discovers that the successful implementation of the recommendation has resulted in a deterioration of his or her social functioning and problem solving skills. Deterioration which follows effective implementation is a good signal that the therapist has made an inaccurate assessment and has given a destructive recommendation based upon the inaccurate assessment (Lantz, 1986B). At this point the therapist should request the client to discontinue the client's attempt to implement the recommendation. The therapist and the client should then move back to the assessment stage. (See figure number four.)

## The Resistance Stage

Like implementation, the resistance stage also follows the prescription recommendation stage. (See figure number four.) In the resistance stage the client blocks the therapist's recommendation through the manifestation of resistance (Lantz, 1986B). Resistance should be considered as a signal from the client to the therapist that there are developmental fears and past experiences which need to be discussed before the client implements the recommendation (Andrews, 1972). It is important for the therapist to respect the client's resistance, to allow the client the opportunity to block the recommendation without receiving signals of anger and frustration from the therapist and to communicate to the client that the therapist realizes that there may be some very good reasons for the client's resistance which should be explored. At this point the therapist and the client move into the clarification stage, and the treatment process moves from being primarily a "here and now" type of treatment towards a treatment form which explores developmental or "there and then" issues (Hollis, 1972) (Lantz, 1986B).

## The Clarification Stage

During the clarification stage of treatment the client and the therapist attempt to explore developmental antecedents of the client's resistance to the prescription recommendation. During this stage of treatment the therapist may find it useful to borrow a number of insight oriented treatment tools from the psychoanalytic treatment orientation. Tools such as dream interpretation, free association, and transference interpretation techniques are often useful in helping the client understand developmental influences contributing to the client's resistance towards the recommendation (Lantz, 1986B) (Lantz, 1986A).

The Gestalt concept of catastrophic expectations can be used as a vehicle to help identify developmental issues creating resistance to adaptive solution patterns. A catastrophic expectation is a client's fantasy about the terrible consequences which could occur if the client implements what the therapist considers to be an adaptive solution (Lantz, 1986B).

The clinical social worker can utilize the concept of catastrophic expectations to help the client identify repressed thoughts, feelings, fears and memories which are triggering and/or mobilizing resistance to the recommendation. In this process the therapist communicates his or her respect for the client's resistance to the client, asks the client to imagine "What bad things might happen if you implement the recommendation?" and then asks the client if the client has any memories of experiencing or observing such "bad things" in the past (Lantz, 1986B). Such an empathic reflection process generally leads to the client's development of insight. At this point the therapist and the client move into the insight stage. (See figure number four.)

## The Insight Stage

During the insight stage of treatment the client will usually become aware of repressed memories from the past which will help the client understand why he or she is resistive to the prescription recommendation. The client also experiences increased awareness about how developmental experiences have contributed to the client's manifestation of his or her primary social movement pattern. Such insight is usually accompanied by the experience of catharsis. As the client is able to remember repressed material, the client will usually ventilate strong feelings which accompany the repressed material. This is usually experienced painfully by the client, yet at the same time such a catharsis provides the client with a sense of relief. These cathartic experiences seem to free the client in a way that lets the client begin to implement the therapist's recommendation (Lantz 1986B). At this point the client and the therapist move back to the prescription recommendation stage and begin to repeat the treatment cycle. (See figure number four.) The following case presentation illustrates work done by a therapist and client during the resistance stage, the clarification stage and the insight stage of treatment.

### The Lyle Case

Mr. Lyle, an aggression deficiency social functioning pattern client, requested treatment because he believed that his inability to be assertive and his fear of competitive situations was holding up his advancement at his place of employment. Mr. Lyle and his therapist developed the treatment contract of working towards including appropriate anger and assertive behavior into Mr. Lyle's social functioning repertoire. The therapist designed a set of interactional recommendations which were directed towards helping Mr. Lyle achieve his primary treatment goal. Mr. Lyle manifested strong resistance to these recommendations and blocked them effectively. The therapist began to help Mr. Lyle reflect on the reasons behind this resistance:

Therapist: It seems to me that you are doing a pretty good job of keeping yourself from applying the suggestions that I have been making. Have you any ideas as to why this is happening?

Client: Not really, I just don't have the time and . . . well you know how it is. You get busy and forget.

Therapist: Yet you are putting time and effort into getting these suggestions and could make time to implement them. I think that there may be some reasons behind this.

Client: Well . . . I'm not really sure.

Therapist: It's been my experience that people don't forget to do what they say they want to do, unless there are some very good reasons for these memory lapses.

Client: You are probably right. (Slightly angry tone)

Therapist: What I would like for you to do is to take a few seconds and just imagine what bad things might happen if you were to implement my suggestions. Kind of brainstorm about all the bad things that could happen. Close your eyes and pretend. What might happen?

Client:     Silence (With eyes closed)

Client:     Well . . . this sounds funny but well . . . I might hurt someone's feelings, or well, I might even just hurt someone (shakey voice).

Therapist:  Hurt someone?

Client:     Well, I might hit someone or . . . you know, lose control. You know I wouldn't want to get violent.

Therapist:  Have you ever gotten violent?

Client:     Well, no.

Therapist:  Never?

Client:     No I never have!

Therapist:  Have you ever seen or observed this kind of thing? Were you ever around it?

Client:     (Crying) Well yes . . . this is strange. I haven't thought about it for years but when I was young my Dad did a lot of drinking. He was an alcoholic. I remember times when he beat my Mom.

Client:     (Silence) (Soft crying)

Client:     I haven't thought of this in years.

Therapist:  Is there any particular incident that you can recall and tell me about?

At this point Mr. Lyle was able to tell the therapist about his experiences watching his father beat his mom. Mr. Lyle talked about his feelings of guilt about not being able to protect his mother. The therapist suggested that Mr. Lyle's failure to be aggressive and/or assertive might well be his way of "protecting people now" in an attempt to "make things up to your mother." This interpretation was useful to Mr. Lyle who used it to free up additional memories about his discomfort in conflict situations. Mr. Lyle was eventually able to use his insights to help him include appropriate aggression within his primary social movement pattern. He was able to implement the therapist's recommendations.

## The Client's Response to the Ten Stage Treatment Cycle

Different kinds of clients have different patterns of response to the ten stage treatment cycle. Fairly healthy clients who suffer from adjustment disorder difficulties or who are experiencing some form of specific problem and crisis situation generally are able to move through the treatment cycle in a rapid fashion. Such clients frequently are able to avoid the resistance side of the treatment cycle. They are often able to move rapidly through joining, assessment, prescription recommendation and implementation to enhancement and termination. Such clients generally spend from a few weeks to three or four months in treatment (Lantz, 1978A) (Lantz, 1986B).

Neurotic clients who request treatment are not generally able to move as rapidly through the treatment cycle. Such clients usually manifest resistance and often need to spend considerable time on the resistance side of the treatment cycle. Such clients can often be expected to spend from three months to one or more years in treatment (Lantz, 1986). Neurotic clients usually need to go through and repeat the treatment cycle at least three or four times. More severely disturbed neurotic clients may need to spend even more time in clinical social work treatment (Lantz, 1986B).

Personality disorder or character disorder clients generally spend from one to four years in treatment. These clients have severely ingrained difficulties and manifest strong resistance to both change and to the treatment process. Such clients need considerable time and help during the joining stage. They are particularly skilled at resisting recommendations. Resistance is almost always a continuing process when working with a personality disorder client (Gedo, 1979) (Masterson, 1976).

The psychotic client and the "all or nothing pattern" client require an extremely long period of time in social work treatment in order to make significant gains. Trust is a significant issue with such clients, and both joining and assessment usually become lengthy stages. Such clients often bolt from treatment and when this occurs the treatment process must always be reinstituted back at the joining stage. Such clients may spend from three to ten years in treatment (Arieti, 1955) (Masterson, 1976) (Lantz, 1986B).

## Eclecticism and the Ten Stage Treatment Cycle

Again, the primary treatment goal in clinical social work treatment is to help the client develop increased flexibility and balance within the client's social functioning pattern. The ten stage treatment cycle provides a flexible, yet consistent, treatment structure which can free the social worker and client to use a wide and rich variety of techniques and treatment modalities to achieve this primary treatment goal. Clinical social workers can use the ten stage treatment cycle as a way to incorporate analytic, behavioral, interactional and reflective techniques in a goal directed fashion. The therapist can also use individual, group, marital and family treatment modalities in a number of different creative combinations without infringing upon the systematic process of treatment (Lantz, 1986B).

## Chapter Five

# CLINICAL SITUATIONS

The clinical social worker is both skeptical and appreciative of the process of clinical diagnosis. Making a diagnosis is both helpful and reductionistic. The client is a person and can never be described fully by any diagnostic label. At the same time an accurate classification of the client's problems can help the clinical practitioner by allowing the practitioner the opportunity to study clinical interventions which have been found helpful with other clients who have similar problems. A more informed decision can then be made whether or not such interventions should be used in the present situation with the present client (APA, 1980) (Gedo, 1979) (Lantz, 1978A).

It is not the purpose of this chapter to completely review the various diagnostic classification systems which have been used to classify client problems. The purpose is instead to add to such systems the viewpoint of a social functioning approach. This will be done through a description of a variety of common clinical situations as well as a description of the intervention possibilities which would often be considered by the practitioner of clinical social work.

## Adjustment Disorders

An adjustment disorder is defined by the American Psychiatric Association's *Diagnostic and Statistical Manual of Mental Disorders* (APA, 1980) as a maladaptive reaction to an identifiable life event or circumstance. An adjustment disorder is not simply an exacerbation of a preexisting mental disorder. The client with an adjustment disorder should improve and return to a healthy level of functioning when the client's stress is removed or ceases to exist. The client's reaction to the stressful circumstances may trigger an impairment in social functioning and symptoms such as anxiety or depression which are in excess of what is considered to be a normal reaction to such a circumstance (APA, 1980).

Anxiety and depression are the two most prominent feeling states which accompany the development of an adjustment disorder. Depres-

121

sion associated with an adjustment disorder is not usually effectively treated by the prescription of antidepressant medications and most practitioners believe that antianxiety medicines should be used conservatively (Lieb and Slaby, 1975). Most authorities agree that the adjustment disorder client can be most effectively helped through the provision of supportive psychotherapy and/or environmental modification (Lieb and Slaby, 1975) (Aguilera and Messick, 1978).

The clinical social worker uses the manifestation of an adjustment disorder as a signal that the client needs to develop a new method of perceiving and evaluating the new social situation (i.e. the triggering event) and/or that the client needs to develop new coping skills and environmental supports in response to the client's changing social situation. Treatment with the adjustment disorder client is usually a short term form of psychotherapy in which the therapist actively directs the client towards the development of new coping skills, new environment supports, and new methods of perceiving and evaluating the self and/or social situation (Lantz, 1978A). At times individual psychotherapy will be used to maximize support from the therapist, and at other times the client will be seen in family treatment to help the client and the family maximize the client's natural network of support. The adjustment disorder client is usually a person who has developed an exaggerated use of the moving towards or away from other people patterns in response to a specific stress. The moving against pattern is rarely found when a client is experiencing an adjustment disorder.

## Antisocial Personality Disorder

The antisocial personality disorder client usually has a long history of continuous and chronic antisocial behavior in which the rights of other people are violated (APA, 1980) (Rowe, 1980). The antisocial client tends to act out conflicts, tends to blame other people for personal problems and tends to act callous (Rowe, 1980). The onset of this problem tends to occur before the age of 15. Such clients are frequently impulsive, unsocialized, destructive, defiant and deceitful. The antisocial personality client is often immature and has been described as being dominated by primative drives (Rowe, 1980). Most authorities agree that the antisocial personality disorder client does not often show a high rate of improvement in psychotherapy (Lieb and Slaby, 1975). The antisocial personality disorder client most frequently uses a moving against other people's social functioning pattern and most frequently experiences the feelings of anger and rage.

The antisocial personality disorder client is usually highly skilled in the process of externalizing responsibility for personal problems. Such clients tend to "get the other guy before he gets me." The antisocial personality disorder client often has good intelligence and can be very charming when this behavior is considered personally useful. The antisocial personality disorder client does not usually request psychotherapy. Treatment is usually requested by such clients when psychotherapy is presented to the client by the judicial system as an alternative to jail. Although treatment with such clients is frequently unsuccessful, successful treatment is still possible. At times such clients respond favorably to a therapist who is somewhat charismatic and who is also comfortable with both anger and limit setting. At times the client can benefit from treatment if the therapist can help the client see that a rigid use of the aggressive pattern is personally damaging to the client. At times the antisocial personality disorder client can benefit from a group therapy experience if feedback from the other group members helps the client realize that antisocial behavior is not helping the client achieve his/her personal goals.

## Anxiety Disorders

The feeling of anxiety is the most prominent symptom experienced in all kinds of anxiety disorders (Rowe, 1980). Symptoms or signals of anxiety include tension, apprehension, panic, avoidance behavior, and at times vigilant behavior (Gray, 1978). Types of anxiety disorders include panic disorders, obsessive compulsive disorders, generalized anxiety disorders, post traumatic stress disorders, and phobic disorders (APA, 1980). Two to four percent of the general population has at one time or another experienced a set of symptoms which could accurately be labeled as an anxiety disorder (Rowe, 1980).

Freudian psychotherapists generally view anxiety disorders as resulting from the individual's unsuccessful attempt to deal with primitive needs (Gray, 1978). In this view the anxiety disorder results from incomplete repression of the primitive drives making the anxiety and avoidance experience manditory (Gray, 1978). Behaviorally oriented psychotherapists frequently view the anxiety disorders as being learned behaviors (Rowe, 1980), and in recent years a number of psychiatrists have stated that the anxiety disorders may well result from a physiological predisposition to anxiety (Rowe, 1980).

The development of an anxiety disorder often indicates that the client has developed a somewhat inflexible use of the avoidance social functioning pattern. In some instances the anxiety disorder client will be found to be using his/her anxiety to obtain the support of significant others. In such instances the client will be using the dependency pattern. These clients seldom present to the clinical practitioner without the manifestation of some depression concurrent with the anxiety.

Although the anxiety disorder client usually exhibits one of two of the above mentioned social functioning patterns, the client almost always has great difficulty expressing angry feelings or acting in an assertive and/or appropriately aggressive fashion. The anxiety disorder client is afraid of anger and aggression. The fear can be about personal aggression and/or the aggression of others.

The therapist should generally attempt to help the anxiety disorder client learn to be more comfortable in the utilization of aggression, assertion and anger. The therapist should provide recommendations to the client that are designed to help the client practice assertive behavior. Clarification and interpretations are used when the client manifests resistance to the recommendation to help the client gain insight into the developmental issues which encourage or trigger the client's avoidance and fear of aggression. Individual, group and family treatment modalities are all frequently found to be useful with the anxiety disorder client, and at times antianxiety medications can be a useful adjunct to treatment (Synder, 1980).

## Avoidant Personality Disorder

The client with an avoidant personality disorder is usually described as being a person who is unwilling to get involved in a relationship with another person unless given exceptional guarantees of total acceptance (Rowe, 1980). Such an individual evidences consistent social withdrawal, yet maintains an internal desire for acceptance and affection (APA, 1980). The avoidant personality disorder client has a low sense of self-esteem and is not able to trust his or her own ability to rebound or adjust to any form of perceived rejection. Such a pattern is usually found to be deeply ingrained and is manifested in a wide variety of social living situations (Gregory and Smeltzer, 1977).

The therapist should generally attempt to provide such clients with a consistent, accepting and nondemanding treatment relationship, at least in the beginning stage of treatment. Such clients generally need to be seen initially in individual psychotherapy. At a later point in treatment the client can often be switched to a group therapy modality. The avoidant personality disorder client is often viewed by the therapist as using an extreme form of the moving away from others social functioning pattern. The therapist's slow, nondemanding, consistent and accepting attitude is the best guarantee of engaging the client in a treatment relationship. The experience of psychotherapy, rather than interpretations or insight seem to be the most helpful ingredient in this type of client's recovery (Lantz, 1978A).

## Bipolar Disorder

The most common form of the bipolar disorder is called manic-depressive illness. Most authorities (Gregory and Smeltzer, 1977) (Lieb and Slaby, 1975) agree that this illness has a significant biochemical component. It is often assumed that the manic-depressive client has a catecholamine imbalance within the central nervous system (Gregory and Smeltzer, 1977) which results in mood swings from depression to mania. Often there is a concurrent thought disorder present with the mood disturbance (Gregory and Smeltzer, 1977). Lithium is a drug that is frequently found to be effective in helping the client control manic-depressive mood swings (Lieb and Slaby, 1975).

The therapist should generally view medication to be the best approach to use in treating the bipolar disorder client. Psychotherapy is often used to help the client adjust to his or her illness and to help the client learn how to prevent episodes of the illness in the future. The bipolar disorder client often utilizes an all or nothing social functioning pattern while having an episode of the illness. Such clients will at times continue this pattern even after the mood disturbance has been controlled through medication. When this occurs, supportive psychotherapy is generally indicated (Lieb and Slaby, 1975). The nonmedical psychotherapist should not treat the bipolar disorder client unless a psychiatrist is involved in the treatment process (Lantz, 1978A).

## Borderline Personality Disorder

The borderline personality disorder client manifests consistent and ongoing instability in a variety of areas including self-image, mood, behavior and interpersonal relationships (Rowe, 1980). The client will usually demonstrate unstable interpersonal relationships, impulsive behavior, inappropriate and overly intense feeling states, confusion about both short and long range goals and confusion about personal identity (AMA, 1980). The borderline personality disorder client frequently utilizes primitive defense mechanisms such as projection and splitting (Rowe, 1980). A number of authorities (Masterson, 1976) (Rowe, 1980) consider the borderline personality disorder client to be a person who has had negative and unsuccessful experiences during the separation-individuation stage of psychosexual development. In this view the disorder is reactive to a situation in the client's family of origin where the client's mother withdrew love and affection as the child began to emotionally separate from the mother. In other words, the client was not encouraged to become a separate person. This original trauma which generally occurs between 18 and 36 months of age, results in ongoing confusion about both identity and interpersonal relationships (Mahler, 1958). The borderline client unfortunately often learns to believe that a relationship with a significant other can only occur through complete emotional fusion (Masterson, 1976). Any individual who attempts to maintain a degree of autonomy and emotional separateness during a relationship with the borderline client will often be viewed by the borderline client as being "dead" or nonexisting as a person. Any hint of separateness, separation or autonomy on the part of the significant other will frequently trigger intense fear and rage within the borderline personality disorder client. The borderline client will then react with extreme aggression, dependency or withdrawal. Separation triggers the fear of total loss for the borderline personality disorder client (Masterson, 1976). On the other hand, the borderline client frequently views his or her own personal growth as separation from the original object and reacts to such growth with guilt and despair. Such attempts at growth on the part of the borderline client often trigger suicidal impulses (Masterson, 1976).

The therapist should view the borderline client as being a person who utilizes an all or nothing social functioning pattern. The client is seen as an extremely insecure person who attempts to obtain total emotional fusion with a significant other. When this occurs, or appears to occur, the significant other is temporarily viewed as totally good. When the significant other manifests a degree of autonomy and separateness the borderline client experiences a fear of total loss of the good object. The client will then strongly react by manifesting an extreme form of aggression, depression and/or anxiety. These dynamics are played out in the relationship with the therapist during the process of treatment.

The therapist can utilize the treatment relationship and the process of treatment as a learning laboratory for the borderline personality disorder client. Insight, support and experiential validation are the curative factors which most frequently can have a positive impact upon the borderline client. The relationship between the client and therapist is structured by the therapist in a way that stimulates those three curative factors and their emergence around the issue of separation-individuation. The therapist remains consistent, caring, concerned, available and autonomous with the borderline client inspite of the client's testing and the extreme patterns which are manifested by the client toward the therapist during treatment. The therapist actively monitors countertransference in a way that prevents destructive acting out on the part of the therapist and the disruption of empathy from the therapist to the client. The therapist consistently reassures the client through work, words and action, that client growth towards autonomy will not trigger rejection from the therapist. Psychotherapy with the borderline client is often difficult and should not be attempted by the beginning practitioner without close supervision by an experienced "veteran." Even the experienced practitioner should not hesitate to utilize supervision or consultation when working with the borderline client.

## Compulsive Personality Disorder

The compulsive personality disorder client has great difficulty expressing warm feelings in his or her interpersonal relationships. Such clients are preoccupied with rules, details and efficiency (APA, 1980). They are often described as stingy, overly conventional, serious, overly concerned with production and inordinately afraid to make a mistake (APA, 1980) (Rowe, 1980). The compulsive personality disorder client stubbornly insists that other people submit to their own way of doing things and such clients are often oppositional when forced to flexibly accept or adjust to the will of others (Rowe, 1980). Psychoanalytic oriented practitioners often view such clients as having had problems in the anal phase of psychosexual development (Gedo, 1979).

The clinical social worker generally views the compulsive personality disorder client as being an individual who uses compulsive behaviors as a method or technique which helps the client move away from other people. The client frequently suffers with anxiety. The compulsive personality disorder client is viewed as an avoiding pattern client because the client's compulsive behaviors are frequently exquisitely successful at alienating other people. Such clients are frequently viewed by many therapists as being good candidates for group psychotherapy. The group treatment experience can be helpful to such clients as it can help them discover how compulsive behaviors interfere with their ability to relate with others (Yalom, 1970).

### Dependent Personality Disorder

The dependent personality disorder client views the self as weak and consistently attempts to get other people to assume responsibility for personal problems and personal difficulties (Rowe, 1980). The dependent personality disorder client will subordinate personal needs to the will of others as a "trade off" which is used to avoid personal responsibility. The client evidences a lack of self confidence and shows considerable discomfort when left alone (APA, 1980). The client often will belittle the self, feel helpless and become submissive in interpersonal relationships (APA, 1980).

Many practitioners (Horney, 1945) view the dependent personality disorder client as bieng a person who exclusively and rigidly utilizes the moving towards other people social functioning pattern. This dependency pattern is built upon the client's poor self concept and the client's skill at getting significant others to "take over." The client often experiences and uses depression to facilitate help from others.

Experienced practitioners will frequently see the dependent pattern client individually during the initial stage of treatment. This helps the client join in treatment by meeting some of the client's dependency needs in the one-to-one relationship. After the client has developed a relationship with the therapist, the therapist will frequently encourage the client to join a therapy group. The dependent pattern client will often find great benefit in group treatment as the modality offers both multiple sources of support and multiple sources of confrontation. This can help the client learn to see the self as having many more strengths than have been previously realized and recognized.

## Dissociative Disorders

According to the American Psychiatric Association's *Diagnostic and Statistical Manual* (APA, 1980) there are four kinds of dissociative disorders: psychogenic amnesia, psychogenic fuge, multiple personality and depersonalization disorder. The essential feature of all four disorders is the temporary alteration of consciousness, identity or motor behavior so that some part of these functions is temporarily lost to awareness (Rowe, 1980). Although such clients exhibit considerable personality disorganization they are not considered psychotic. In these disorders the client uses dissociation to compartmentalize a component of thinking, feeling and/or motor activity in a way that appears to be beyond the client's control (Rowe, 1980). Psychoanalytic practitioners frequently believe that in such disorders the client's ego is protecting the client from overwhelming anxiety reactive to some form of perceived trauma (Kolb, 1977). The trauma can be from either the client's past or present psychosocial situation (Kolb, 1977).

Many therapists view the dissociative disorder client as being a person who is distancing a part of the self from another part of the self. In other words, the client's ego is moving away from a part of the person's social living experience. The dissociative experience may represent the ego's movement away from conflicts from the past or from the awareness of problems and/or traumas in the present situation. Often the therapist's primary task is to offer the client enough support so that the client can move towards, and work through, the repressed material and/or the present trauma situation. In terms of classical social casework practice this is called lending the client the therapist's ego (Hollis, 1977). In most instances individual psychotherapy is the modality of choice when working with the dissociative disorder client. At times group or family treatment can be used as an adjunct to the individual modality. Individual psychotherapy is useful in this clinical situation because it maximizes ongoing reliable support and encourages internal reflection.

## Histrionic Personality Disorder

The histrionic personality disorder client has been described as engaging in behavior that is exhibitionistic, theatrical, overly reactive, insincere, superficial, flirtatious, vain, egocentric and self-absorbed (APA, 1980) (Rowe, 1980). The disorder is most frequently found in females and has been described as possibly being a feminine form of antisocial personality disorder (Celani, 1976). This view suggests that there is a significant cultural and learning component involved in the disorder (Kalb, 1977).

The experienced practitioner generally views the histrionic personality disorder client as being a person who uses a moving against others social functioning pattern. The client is viewed as using a theatrical and flirtatious type of aggression to manipulate others in a way which ensures their continued interest inspite of the fact that they are consistently being used by the histrionic client. Experienced practitioners will often use treatment techniques with the histrionic client which are very similar to the treatment techniques utilized when working with the antisocial personality disorder client. Young male therapists should not work with the histrionic personality disorder client without close supervision. This helps protect both the client and the therapist from the possibility of seduction.

## Impulse Control Disorders

Like the antisocial personality disorder client, the impulse control disorder client also engages in antisocial behavior (Gray, 1978). The antisocial personality disorder client engages in antisocial behavior in a wide variety of situations. The impulse control disorder client is different in that the impulse control disorder client engages in such behaviors in a limited and narrow set of psychosocial situations. The impulse disorder client engages in a repitition expression of a single pleasurable but antisocial impulse (APA, 1980). The impulse disorder client is generally considered to be acting out a neurotic conflict where the antisocial personality disorder is considered to be demonstrating an antisocial style of general living (Rowe, 1980). The impulse control disorder client generally experiences an increased sense of internal tension and then gives into the tension by failing to resist the drive and then acting out the tension (Rowe, 1980). Acting out behaviors can include gambling, stealing, fire setting or explosive aggression (Rowe, 1980). A neurological work-up is often helpful to such clients.

The impulse control disorder client can often be helped through insight oriented psychotherapy. In this form of treatment the client is encouraged to talk out conflicts and to learn to dissipate and resist mounting tension through the process of verbalization. In many instances the nature of the impulsive behavior has symbolic significance. The realization of this symbolic significance by the client will often short circuit the need for the antisocial behavior (Gray, 1978).

## Introverted Personality Disorder

The introverted personality disorder client has also been labeled as having a schizoid personality (APA, 1980). Such clients have great difficulty forming and/or maintaining social relationships. They frequently exhibit a bland affect, act reserved, are withdrawn and act seclusive (Rowe, 1980). Such clients often pursue solitary interests and have problems expressing both hostility and warmth. They often appear self-absorbed and frequently engage in autistic thinking (Rowe, 1980) (APA, 1980). Such clients generally have little desire for social involvement and treatment is often unsuccessful (Kubie, 1936) (Krill, 1968).

Experienced practitioners often view the introverted personality disorder client as being a person who has learned to maximize anxiety and use a moving away from other people social functioning pattern. Such clients usually become engaged in treatment reactive to a crisis situation in which an external event, such as a promotion at work, makes it impossible for the client to continue using his or her primary social movement pattern (Krill, 1968). In such situations the client becomes overwhelmed with anxiety and may request mental health services. In some instances such a crisis situation may trigger the emergence of an underlying psychosis (Raymond, Slaby and Lieb, 1975).

The clinical social worker will generally attempt to help such clients by using environmental modification techniques to assist the client in the client's efforts to minimize the interpersonal demands placed upon the client by the emergence of the new psychosocial situation. The therapist attempts to become a friend who helps the client minimize external social demands and in this way enters into the client's life. The therapist respects the client's need for minimal human involvement but paradoxically pairs this respect for the client's defenses with the emergence of a therapeutic friendship (Krill, 1969). The therapist becomes a person who knows how to help the client minimize anxiety and in this way helps the client open the door for the beginning of a human relationship. In many instances the client will view this no demand approach to friendship on the part of the therapist as "the exception to the rule" and will let the therapist enter the client's life in a way that has never previously occurred. This beginning treatment relationship is nurtured by sporadic individual treatment sessions. At a later point in treatment the client is encouraged to enter into a therapy group. Such clients require much patience on the part of the therapist before they can honestly commit themselves to the goal of changing their well practiced style of isolated social living.

## Narcissistic Personality Disorder

The narcissistic personality disorder client usually exhibits extreme self-centeredness, self-absorption, a consistent need for attention and admiration, a lack of empathy for other people and a grandiose sense of self importance (APA, 1980). Such clients usually exploit others to obtain personal gratification (Rowe, 1980). Such clients are in many ways similar to the antisocial personality disorder client but are also different in that they seldom actually violate the law. The narcissistic personality disorder client feels comfortable using others but is extremely uncomfortable about taking chances that risk incarceration.

Such clients seldom request psychotherapy, and when such a request is made it is usually reactive to a situation in which significant others have decided to no longer reinforce the client's self centeredness. The change in attitude by the narcissistic personality disorder client's significant others triggers depression in the client. The client requests psychotherapy to help get things back to the way "they used to be," or to "help me get these people off my back."

The experienced practitioner often views the narcissistic personality disorder client as having the best chance for a successful treatment experience in the group therapy modality. Group treatment can help such clients learn how their own actions destroy positive relationships with other people. The therapist will attempt to help such clients learn that it is in their own best interest to change their own social functioning pattern in a way that is less destructive to others.

## Organic Mental Disorders

An organic mental disorder is considered to be a transient or permanent brain dysfunction caused by the destruction or damage of nerve cells in the central nervous system (APA, 1980). A chronic organic mental disorder occurs when the damage to the nerve cells is permanent and results in a permanent dysfunction. An acute orgnic mental disorder occurs when the damage to the nerve cells is reversible, or when the effects of the damage are reversible. Types of organic disorders include senile and presenile dementias, substance induced organic disorders, organic disorders reactive to endocrine dysfunction, organic disorders reactive to metabolic and electrolytic abnormalities, organic disorders reactive to nutritional deficiency, organic disorders reactive to infections or viral diseases, orgnic disorders reactive to vascular disorders, organic disorders reactive to brain tumors or brain trauma, and organic disorders reactive to toxic conditions (Rowe, 1980).

The type of treatment recommended for the organic mental disorder client depends upon the cause of the tissue damage. Treatment is directed at the underlying cause of the dysfunction and depends upon an accurate assessment of the factor or factors which are causing the damage. Such treatment should be provided by a practitioner of the medical profession. If the damage is reversible, psychotherapy is often not necessary. If the damage is permanent, the task of the therapist becomes to help the client develop realistic expectations about what the client can or cannot accomplish in view of the organic damage. At times retraining programs can be helpful, and at other times custodial care must be organized and utilized. Individual and/or family treatment can often be useful to the client and the client's family by helping them work through grief feelings about the brain tissue damage.

## Passive-aggressive Personality Disorder

The passive-aggressive personality disorder client has been described as a person who passively resists, resents and opposes any demands made by significant others to either increase or maintain a given level of functioning (APA, 1980) (Rowe, 1980). Such clients express this resistance indirectly through procrastination, intentional inefficiency and selective forgetfulness.

Many therapists view the passive-aggressive client as having or using an aggression-deficiency social functioning pattern. The client is viewed as being uncomfortable and afraid of aggression and angry feelings. The client will then express this aggression in a passive manner which protects the client from an awareness of his or her own personal feelings of aggression and anger. Since such a pattern tends to "drive other people up a wall" the client will frequently experience angry feelings from other people and will generally be surprised and shocked that "people get mad at me."

The passive-aggressive personality disorder client can generally be helped in group psychotherapy. The group modality offers the passive-aggressive client the opportunity to specifically learn "why other people get so mad at me." The client's passive-aggressive behaviors can be spotted in the group therapy experience, and the client can receive feedback about such behaviors as they occur in the here and now of the group therapy process. Such feedback can result in insight and the development of the client's will to change.

## Psychophysiologic Disorders

The term psychophysiologic disorders refers to a group of disorders which are characterized by physical symptoms which are caused primarily by emotional difficulties (Rowe, 1980). Such disorders usually involve one specific organ system and are triggered by neurotic emotional conflict (Gray, 1978). Such emotional conflict can trigger dysfunctional gastrointestinal reactions, cardiovascular reactions, respitory disorders, musculoskeletal disorders and skin disorders (Kolb, 1977). Anxiety seems to be a primary component in all of the psychophysiologic disorders (Rowe, 1980) (Kolb, 1977) (Alexander, 1950).

The clinical social work practitioner often views the psychophysiologic disorder client to be a person who utilizes an avoiding social functioning pattern. The client's physical symptoms are viewed as a physical form of anxiety and an effort is made to determine what situation or situations are being avoided through the manifestation of the physical problem. Treatment generally includes the monitoring of the physical problem by a medical practitioner, supportive psychotherapy designed to help the client recognize and talk out the underlying anxiety that is triggering the physical problem, and encouragement to confront the situation which is being avoided.

## Schizophrenic Disorders

Schizophrenia is a term which identifies a large group of psychiatric disorders frequently characterized by problems in thought, perception, feelings, behavior and communication which lasts longer than six months (APA, 1980). Bleuler (1950) describes four main symptoms of schizophrenia which are a disturbance of affect, a disturbance of association, autism, and abnormal ambivalence. Other symptoms frequently found in schizophrenia include social functioning disorganization, communication disorganization, delusions, hallucinations, loss of ego boundaries, withdrawal, catatonic posturing, eccentric appearance, ideas of reference, and illusions (Lieb and Slaby, 1975). The cause of schizophrenia is still unknown but most authorities (Lieb and Slaby, 1975) (Snyder, 1980) (Gregory and Smeltzer, 1977) believe that schizophrenia results from a combination of both biological and sociocultural factors. The author's approach to the treatment of schizophrenia has been discussed and illustrated extensively in Chapter Three.

## Somatoform Disorders

A somatoform disorder is a neurotic problem in which physical symptoms with no known physiological mechanisms are present and linked with psychological conflict (APA, 1980). The four types of somatoform disorders are somatization disorder, conversion disorder, psychogenic pain disorder, and hypochondriasis (Rowe, 1980). The symptom of anxiety seems to be frequently associated with the development of a somatoform disorder.

Most therapists view the client with a somatoform disorder as being similar to the psychophysiologic disorder client and generally attempt to use supportive psychotherapy to help the client talk through the underlying conflicts which are triggering the development of the disorder. Again, medical monitoring of the physical symptoms and support to the client for confronting the triggering psychosocial situation are important ingredients in treatment.

## Substance Abuse Disorders

A substance abuse disorder occurs when a person becomes dependent or abuses the use of a substance that modifies the person's mood or behavior (APA, 1980) (Rowe, 1980). Substance abuse can occur through the use of alcohol, barbituates, cocaine, opioids, amphetamines, cannabis, tabacco, and other toxic drugs. Although there are many different theories about the etiology of substance abuse, most authorities believe that the disorder is caused by a combination of factors including stress, cultural factors, psychological factors and a genetic predisposition towards the illness (Jellinek, 1960).

There is no single social functioning pattern associated with substance abuse difficulties. The addictive component of many of the abused substances may lead to a criminal, dependent, or manipulative style of social living. Such a style of living develops in reaction to the abusers need to pay for drugs, or to compensate for a deteriorating ability to live up to ordinary social demands. Denial on the part of the substance abuse client and his or her family and friends is a frequent occurrence. Treatment is often not requested until the client has run out of money, friends and family members who are willing to trade support for the stated good intentions of the substance abusing client. When the substance abuse client has used up all of his or her support systems, the client will "crash" and at this point is often truly motivated for treatment. Group and family therapy approaches to treatment are frequently found useful. Self help organizations such as Alcoholics Anonymous and Narcotics Anonymous are probably the most effective form of help that has yet been developed (Mendelson, 1966).

## Unipolar Depression Disorders

A unipolar depression is a form of depression that is not followed by a manic episode or preceeded by a manic episode (Kolb, 1977). Symptoms of unipolar depression often include disturbed sleep, disturbed appetite, somatic delusions, reality distortions, the inability to experience pleasure, retarded motor activity, and a loss of the person's usual interst in activities (Gregory and Smeltzer, 1977). Unipolar depression can occur on either a psychotic or nonpsychotic level of intensity. It can be reactive or endogenous in nature and can have physiological, psychological and/or social components (Rowe, 1980). The person who suffers with depression should always be considered to be at risk for suicide. Unipolar depression is a common psychiatric problem, and it is estimated that thirty percent of the population has had at least one episode of depression during their lifetime (Rowe, 1980). Most forms of depression respond well to treatment and most practitioners agree that a pluralistic approach to treatment is usually indicated (Rowe, 1980).

The psychosocial therapist will generally view the depressed client as a person who experiences symptoms which encourage the person to use a moving towards other people social functioning pattern. Intense depression appears to trigger feelings of dependency and intense dependency feelings seem to trigger depression.

The nonmedical psychotherapist will usually refer the depressed client for a psychiatrist consultation. At times what looks like a depression can in reality be a symptom of a nonpsychiatric medical problem. In many instances the prescription of an antidepressant medication can be of great help to the depressed client. If the client is suicidal, psychiatric hospitalization may be necessary. Supportive psychotherapy is also frequently quite helpful to the depressed client. Such an approach should attempt to help the client improve his or her self-esteem, should encourage the client to remain active and to refuse to let the feelings of depression control the client's life, should confront the depressed client's tendency towards regression and dependency, and should help the client actively maintain the use of realistic external systems of support.

## Family Clinical Situations

The previously described clinical situations have been outlined from an individual frame of reference. Such descriptions exclude the family context of symptom development and encourage the clinical practitioner to view individual or group psychotherapy as the predominant treatment modality. In reality, individual symptoms are often reactive to a family situation which encourages and/or reinforces the development of such symptoms. The remaining part of this chapter will describe a number of family situations which can trigger the manifestation of individual problems and symptoms. The description of such family situations is meant to encourage the clinical practitioner to view family treatment as frequently indicated and often a highly effective form of treatment.

## The Functional Family Group

In the functional family the coalition between the parents is the strongest communication pathway in the family group (Glick and Kessler, 1974). Although the parents are open and available for communiction with the children the parental dyad always remains the strongest subsystem within the family.

In this type of family the parents direct the growth and functioning of the total family unit. The parents act as a team and although they encourage and are respectful of input from the children, the parents do not abandon their responsibility for providing direction and stability to the total family. The functional family system seldom needs mental health services. When such a request is made it is generally reactive to some form of crisis situation such as death of a family member, the loss of a wage earner's job, or the development of a medical crisis by a family member. The development of a functional family system is often considered to be a family therapy intervention goal by many practitioners of the modality (Glick and Kessler, 1974) (Andrews, 1974) (Lantz, 1986C).

## The Schismatic Family Group

In the schismatic family the marital coalition is extremely weak and strong alliances are developed between the parents and the children. In this type of family the parents do not work with each other to provide direction and stability for the children. The children often become the parents' "friend" and the children may gain more power in the family than is developmentally appropriate (Glick and Kessler, 1974). In many instances the parents become depressed and the children are forced to "nurture" the parents. Such a job inhibits the child's natural drive towards autonomy and independence. The child may develop an identity disturbance or the child may "act out" in an effort to get the parents to "pull together" to solve the child's problem.

Family intervention with the schismatic family is directed towards breaking down the overly intense coalitions between parents and children and is also directed towards strengthening the bond between the parents. Family therapy frequently evolves into marital therapy when the parents realize how they have been using the children and when the parents realize that it might be possible to "nurture" each other.

## The Skewed Family Group

In the skewed family group there is a strong coalition between three family members while one family member is isolated from the rest of the family group. The isolated family member can be from either the parental or child generation. The isolated family member is used as a scapegoat by the rest of the family members and all family problems are blamed on the isolated member (Glick and Kessler, 1974). The isolated family member frequently experiences feelings of depression. If the isolated family member is an adult he or she may develop substance abuse difficulties. If the isolated member is an adolescent the adolescent may turn for support to a delinquent peer group.

Treatment with the skewed family group focuses upon helping the isolated family member rejoin the group. If the isolated member can be helped to rejoin the group there is often a fairly immediate and reactive manifestation of marital conflict between the two parents. This suggests that the skewed family structure may well be a family defense used by the family to prevent conflict within the parental generation. Again, marital therapy often evolves as the primary treatment modality reactive to the manifestation of parental marital conflict (Andrews, 1974). Both the skewed and the schismatic family group structures are sometimes called fused family structures (Lantz, 1978A).

## The Generation Gap Family Group

In the generation gap family, the parents have a strong and stable coalition with each other but there is little interaction between the parents and the children (Glick and Kessler, 1974). The parents know how to nurture each other but are not able to nurture the children. In many instances the parents will arrange for the placement of their children into a substitute family situation in order to let other people nurture the children. If the parents are financially well off the children may be placed in a boarding school. If the parents are poor the local children's service agency will often be utilized.

The primary treatment goal when working with the generation gap family is to teach the parents how to parent their children. If the parents are unable to learn, or are extremely resistant to such learning, placement of the children often does become indicated. In many instances the parents can learn to nurture and enjoy their children and placement becomes unnecessary.

## The Pseudodemocratic Family Group

In the pseudodemocratic family no one is in charge. Every family member has equal power. The parents have abandoned their leadership role to the chaotic structure of equality with children who are not developmentally ready for such a task. In this type of family system the children act out in order to structure the parents into a leadership role. The parents often react by increasing their attempts to be democratic and a vicious circle frequently is the result (Glick and Kessler, 1974).

The primary treatment goal when working with this form of family structure is to help the parents act like parents. After some initial resistance the parents usually find that both the children and the parents themselves are quite relieved that someone is finally in charge (Lantz, 1978A) (Lantz, 1986C).

## The Disengaged Family Group

In the disengaged family group the family members are emotionally distant from each other and in most instances are also geographically distant from each other. Such families generally do not stick together and the children often need a substitute family living experience. The disengaged family is seldom helped in family treatment simply because it is almost impossible to get all family members together at one time and in one place. At times members of a family subsystem can be helped to become emotionally close with each other but helping the family as a total group is most often highly unrealistic. Clients who originally were part of a disengaged family can frequently utilize group psychotherapy to make up for a part of their original loss (Lantz, 1978A).

## Summary

Clinical diagnosis is both helpful and dangerous. Although an accurate diagnosis can point to intervention possibilities which could be useful, the fact remains that every client is different and that proper intervention will always depend upon the therapist's ability to relate to the client as a totally unique and individual person. Diagnostic labels are always reductionistic and can be used to hurt the client unless they are utilized with a sense of skepticism and a big grain of salt (Lantz, 1986C).

## Chapter Six

# CLINICAL SOCIAL WORK AND EXISTENTIALISM

Existential philosophers consistently agree that the central human concern is to actively make or find meaning in human existence (Friedman, 1964). For Kierkegaard (1954) the key concept in finding meaning is interest. The Latin "interesse" suggests being between, involved and "in it" rather than standing on the outside. For Buber (1937) (1947) such interest occurs in the dialogue between "I and you" which is the antithesis of disconnectedness and alienation. Camus (1942) deplores the plight of the outsider who remains a stranger to both the self and to others. Both Erikson (1959) and Frankl (1969) (1979) have noted that the more a person can authentically relate to another, the easier it is for the person to authentically relate to the self. Frankl (1969), Yalom (1980) and Andrews (1979) all agree that interpersonal relatedness and engagement is most often the therapeutic answer to meaninglessness. Frankl (1969) defines a major purpose of psychotherapy as being the task of helping the client discover meaning in his or her existence. His approach to treatment is called "Logotherapy" or "Meaning therapy" (Frankl, 1969). The central idea in logotherapy is that meaning does exist under all circumstances and that the desire to find meaning is a primary and basic motivation for most human behavior. This view accepts that we do have the freedom to find meaning in our existence and that when we fail to find such meaning there is a resulting existential vacuum. The human being will always fill this existential vacuum. The vacuum can be filled by either a developing sense of meaning or by psychiatric and existential symptoms such as anxiety, depression, despair, confusion and the experience of anomie. From a logotherapy standpoint, a primary goal in most helping relationships is to help the client find meaning in his or her own life and existential situation. This fills the existential vacuum and limits the opportunity for the development of symptoms (Frankl, 1965) (Fabry, 1968) (Lantz, 1986C).

## The Three Aspects of Meaning

There are three aspects to meaning which are the meaning of life, the will to meaning and the freedom to will (Frankl, 1969). Frankl (1965) does believe that life has meaning. In holding this view, he is at odds with many other existential thinkers who believe that life does not have meaning but that human beings can decide to act as if life does have meaning (Spiegelberg, 1972). Frankl (1969) accepts the view that life does have meaning and that this meaning can be discovered in many different ways that are unique to each individual person.

A second aspect of Frankl's thinking about meaning is his concept of the will to meaning. The will to meaning is the primary and basic motivation for most human behavior. All people have a desire to find meaning in their lives and this desire is found in all civilizations, cultures and under all conditions of human living (Frankl, 1965) (Lantz, 1986C).

In addition to believing that life has meaning and that all people have a desire to find this meaning, logotherapists also believe that the human being has the freedom of will to find meaning in his or her existence. In this sense logotherapists oppose the strict determinism of Freud (Fabry, 1968). Frankl (1965) feels that the human being can use the spiritual part of the self to rise above the effects of instincts, environment and the influence of the past. This ability is called the defiant power of the human spirit (Frankl, 1965).

## The Tragic Triad and Human Values

All human beings must face three existential problems which Frankl (1965) calls the tragic triad. These problems are death, suffering and guilt. All people must die and all people must suffer before they die, and all people must at some time in their life face the responsibility they have in living and the existential guilt associated with the fact that no person is capable of completely fulfilling their responsibility to life at all times. These three existential problems are universal and can only be overcome if the person is able to find meaning in his or her death, suffering, and existential guilt (Frankl, 1969).

Three categories of values can help people find meaning in life and in the three existential problems of life. These types of values are creative values, experiential values and attitudinal values (Frankl, 1969). Creative values allow us to find meaning in what we create through the activities of work, hobbies or a commitment to a cause. Experiential values help us to find meaning through what we experience in nature, art and human relationships. Attitudinal values are humanistic attitudes that we may develop and that we can use to help us find meaning even in response to tragic situations (Lantz, 1986C).

### Three Human Dimensions and Antireductionism

Frankl (1975) points out that there are three dimensions of human existence which are the physical dimension, the psychosocial dimension and spiritual dimension. In this view it is impossible to understand human behavior unless we study and treat all three of these human dimensions. Although it is true that the human being is an animal and that a biological understanding of the animal is important, if we deny the spiritual aspect, we reduce the human being to a position where he or she is "nothing but" an animal. In the same manner it is important to understand the psychosocial dimension of human behavior. Yet if we ignore the spiritual dimension, the human is again reduced to where he or she is "nothing but" a psychosocial machine that can be manipulated. Frankl (1969) believes that this tendency to reduce human beings to "nothing but" was a direct influence upon the rise of Hitler and that today this trend is resulting in pollution, increased crime, more frequent suicide and a general disrespect for the importance of human beings and human life.

### The Unconscious, Tension and Happiness

Frankl (1975) accepts Freud's view of the unconscious but has added to Freud's concept a spiritual component. Frankl (1975) believes that the self does not yield to total self-awareness and that much human behavior is based upon unconscious ideas and decisions which are rationalized in the conscious level of awareness at a later point in time. Frankl (1975) and Fabry (1968) both believe that the unconscious includes two components which are the instinctual unconscious and the spiritual or "noetic" unconscious. Fabry (1986) has suggested that the instinctual unconscious includes repressed sexual desires and aggressiveness, and that the spiritual unconscious includes many of our positive qualities such as love and transcendence which we have ignored and failed to recognize. Whereas

Freudian therapists use free association to help clients discover their instinctual unconscious, logotherapists use a "Socratic" dialogue to help clients discover their noetic unconscious (Fabry, 1968) (Lantz, 1982B) (Lantz, 1986C).

Two additional important ideas found in logotherapy are the importance of tension and happiness as a side product. First, Frankl, (1969) points out that tension is a natural part of human existence and that equilibrium does not result in mental health. Equilibrium, is the adjustment to life as it is and often results in a loss of a person's awareness of meaning. On the other hand, disequilibrium is a reaching out to life as "it could be." The tension between life as it is, and life as it could be, strengthens our spiritual muscles. Franlk (1969) also points out that whenever a person directly attempts to find happiness, the person will fail and become unhappy. In logotherapy happiness is a by product of a meaningful life. The only way to obtain happiness is to replace the search for happiness with a search for meaning. In this sense, self transcendence and meaningful values are the only way towards personal human happiness (Frankl, 1969) (Fabry, 1968) (Ackerman, 1958).

## Clinical Social Work and the Problem of Meaning

If Frankl (1969), and other existential thinkers (Camus, 1942), (Andrews, 1979), (Fabry, 1968), and (Buber, 1947) are correct, an absence of meaning or the lack of an awareness of meaning, will consistently result in the development of psychiatric and/or existential symptoms. Frankl (1965), Andews (1979), Buber (1947), Sartre (1946), Yalom (1980), and almost every other existential thinker consider true human engagement to be the person's most effective immunization against meaninglessness. The concept of engagement includes a leap into commitment and action for the benefit of other people (Yalom, 1980). Such commitment and action can be directed towards benefitting specific significant others or the human race in general. Such a commitment to action always includes a sense of self transcendence (Frankl, 1965). Transcendence is different than masochism in that to care deeply about another individual is intrinsically enriching and can only result in a sense of meaning which protects the human spirit from the often brute facts of every day existence (Frankl, 1969) (Fabry, 1968) (Yalom, 1980). In Frankl's terms the experiential values to be found in human relationships can protect us from the existential vacuum (Frankl, 1969) (Lantz, 1986C).

Clinical social work is solidly based upon the existential concept of meaning. Meaning and healthy social functioning have a close and reciprocal relationship (Lantz, 1982B) (Lantz, 1986C). The person's awareness of meaning can stimulate healthy social functioning which, in turn, can stimulate an increased awareness of meaning. On the other hand, a lack of awareness of meaning can stimulate dysfunctional social functioning which, in turn, can then further cloud the individual's sense of meaning (Lantz, 1982B). Dysfunctional social functioning will result in a cycle of despair, and healthy social functioning results in a cycle of growth (Andrews, 1979) (Lantz, 1982B) (Lantz, 1986C).

## Meaning Through Social Functioning Change

A primary goal in clinical social work is to help the client discover meaning in life through a change in the client's social functioning patterns. A second goal is to help the client develop a sense that every moment provides the person with the opportunity to discover what Frankl (1969) calls the unique meaning of the presenting situation.

Barnes (1959) in her analysis of humanistic existentialism points out that bad faith in human relations is generally based upon the use of one of three fundamental positions of existence. She points out that a person may attempt to deny through domination the freedom of the other, that a person may avoid his or her own responsibility and freedom by prostrating the self before the other, and that a person may prevent human contact through isolation by deciding in advance that both the self and no one else is worthy of such contact (Barnes, 1959). Each position is reactive to the experience of bad faith and meaninglessness and in a circular fashion also contributes to the experience of meaninglessness (Barnes, 1959). Barnes (1959), points out that flexibility is one method of preventing the experience of bad faith. The interactional positions outlined by Barnes (1959) are remarkably similar to Horney's (1945) categories of moving against, towards and away from other people. The clinical social work goal of helping the client develop a balanced social functioning pattern which includes a fairly equal reliance upon all three patterns of movement is highly compatible with the idea of confronting bad faith and/or meaninglessness through the use of flexibility (Barnes, 1959). Such flexibility can help prevent the split between subject and object (Barnes, 1959) or in the symbols of Camus (1980) it can prevent the becoming of either a "victim or an executioner."

## Commitment Through Action in Clinical Social Work

Clinical social work is also solidly based upon the existential concept of commitment through action. Andrews (1979) calls such a commitment "growth by existential realization." Existential realization occurs as the client is learning to choose to relinquish resistance to responsible interaction through experience during the treatment relationship (Andrews, 1979). In this view, the process of change is considered a relationship experience rather than just an explanation. Existential realization includes six ideas which follow. Everything includes a limitation, but choice is always included within such limitations. A choice includes an action. A failure to make a choice is a choice to avoid action. All conflicts from the past are also present decisions about the self and others. Change is a process of consistent choosing and rechoosing. Change is possible.

## The Person of the Therapist

A central issue in both clinical social work and existential psychotherapy is the manner in which the client and the therapist are together. The therapist's presence can both facilitate and/or minimize opportunities for engagement in the treatment relationship. If engagement occurs the client increases his or her opportunity to find meaning in both his or her interactions with the therapist and in interactions with significant others. If engagement does not occur the client has less opportunity to find such meaning (Buber, 1947).

If the therapist has an influence upon the client's opportunity to discover engagement and meaning, the form of the therapist's relationship presentations to the client becomes important. Certain assumptions about the therapist's presentations seem consistent and compatible in both clinical social work and existential psychotherapy. These assumptions include: a commitment to authentic communication on the part of the therapist is important in effective psychotherapy; the role of the therapist can never be divested of it's essential humanness; and the therapist is similar to the client in his/her ultimate concerns (Lantz, 1985C).

## A Commitment to Authentic Communication

The clinical social worker views the treatment process as a joint venture between the therapist and the client directed toward the development of increased flexibility and effectiveness within the client's life. The therapist views the treatment task as including active participation towards assisting the client in the client's efforts towards change. The relationship between the therapist and the client is a relationship problem solving process. The therapist's participation in this process is most effective when the therapist models a balanced social functioning movement pattern. Such a pattern is similar to Buber's (1958) "I and thou" relationship and can only occur through the active use of the therapist's subjective response to the client during the experience of directly working with the client. Andrews (1979) notes that authentic interaction between the client and the therapist is most likely to occur when the therapist is active, innovative, candid, provocative, directive, instigating, supportive, encouraging, explicit, intrusive, engaging, observant, clarifying, optimistic, experiential, and confrontive.

## The Role of the Therapist Always Remains a Human Role

Mullan and Sangiuliano (1964) point out that meaningful communication between the client and the therapist depends upon the therapist's acceptance that the evolving person of the therapist is a vital dynamic for effective therapy. Strupp (1959) has pointed out that the therapist's personality is a potent factor in therapeutic action. Mullan and Sangiuliano (1964) feel that the therapist's realization that he or she can never be fully trained or completely knowledgeable permits psychotherapy it's fundamental creativity. The therapist's willingness to change may well be the therapist's best asset in the helping of another human being. The therapist's potential to help is intimately linked with his or her changing relationship to the self, others and the world at large (Mullan and Sangiuliano, 1964). An effective psychotherapist cannot be just a programmed set of technological responses to the client's pain (Andrews, 1979) (Frankl, 1969) (Mullan and Sangiuliano, 1964).

## The Ultimate Concerns of the Therapist are Similar to the Client's Ultimate Concerns

Sullivan (1946) has noted that the client and the therapist are at a basic level more similar than they are different. Frankl (1969), Camus (1955), Andrews (1979) and others have pointed out that every human being must face tragedy, despair, death, suffering, and anxiety. Such feelings and situations cannot be evaded or permanently changed.

The presence of such human tragedy in the life of *both* the client and the therapist is of significant consequence to the outcome to treatment (Mullan and Sangiuliano, 1964). The recognition and acceptance of tragedy on the part of both the client and the therapist can lead to engagement and transcendence. The denial of human tragedy cheats both the client and the therapist in that it prevents the authenticity between the therapist and client which is based upon their common responsibility of finding meaning in an often chaotic universe. The therapist's responsibility for entering the client's life in a way that promotes the client's growth can only occur when the therapist recognizes a basic common bond between the self of the therapist and the self of the client (Lantz, 1985B). This common bond is different than superficial identification. It can only exist in conjunction with the therapist's realization of tragedy in human existence and the therapist's willingness to find meaning in all life inspite of such tragedy and human pain (Lantz, 1985C). The therapist's vigorous yes to life as it really is, is experienced by the client as a core and basic sense of permission to grow (Farber, 1957) (Lantz, 1985C).

## Summary

Existential psychotherapy and clinical social work share a number of basic ideas. These shared ideas include: the importance of finding meaning in human existence, the effectiveness of human engagement in the search for meaning, the importance of authentic communication during the treatment process, and the basic existential similarities between the therapist and the client. Both the existential psychotherapist and the clinical social worker would agree with Gibron (1923) that joy is sorrow unmasked and that faith cannot be separated from it's actions.

# REFERENCES

Ackerman, N., (1958). *The Psychodynamics of Family Life.* New York: Basic Books.

Adler, A. (1927). *The Practice and Theory of Individual Psychology.* New York: Harcourt-Brace and Company.

Aguilera, D. and Messick, J. (1978). *Crisis Intervention.* St. Louis: C.V. Mosby.

Alexander, F. (1950). *Psychosomatic Medicine.* New York: W.W. Norton.

A.P.A. (1980). *Diagnostic and Statistical Manual of Mental Disorders. (Third Edition).* Washington, D.C.: American Psychiatric Association.

Anastasi, A. (1976). *Psychological Testing.* New York: MacMillan.

Anderson, C., Hogarty, G. and Reiss, D. (1980). "Family Treatment of Adult Schizophrenic Patients: A Psycho-Educational Approach." *Schizophrenia Bulletin.* Vol. 6, pp. 490–505.

Andrews, E. (1965). "Identity Maintenance Operations and Group Therapy Process." *International Journal of Group Psychotherapy.* Vol. 15, pp. 491–499.

Andrews, E. (1972). "Therapeutic Interaction in Adult Therapy Groups." In Dedrich, C. and Dye, A. (Eds.). *Group Procedures: Purposes, Processes and Outcomes.* Boston: Houghton-Mifflin.

Andrews, E. (1973). "Family Therapy." In *Group Therapy for the Adolescent.* Brandes, N. and Gradner, M. (Eds.). New York: Jason Aronson.

Andrews, E. (1974). *The Emotionally Disturbed Family.* New York: Jason Aronson.

Andrews, E. (1979). "Understanding and Working with Family Units." In Eisenberg, S. and Patterson, L. (Eds.). *Helping Clients with Special Concerns.* Chicago: Rand McNally.

Ansbacher, H. (1947). "Adlers Place Today in the Psychology of Memory." *Individual Psychological Bulletin.* Vol. 6, pp. 32–40.

Arieti, S. (1955). *Interpretation of Schizophrenia.* New York: Brunner-Mazel.

Bakan, P. (1969). "Hypnotizability, Laterality of Eye Movements and Functional Brain Asymmetry." *Perceptual and Motor Skills.* Vol. 28, pp. 927–932.

Barnes, H. (1959). *Humanistic Existentialism.* Lincoln: University of Nebraska Press.

Basch, M. (1980). *Doing Psychotherapy.* New York: Basic Books.

Biestek, F. (1957). *The Casework Relationship.* Chicago: Loyola University Press.

Bleuler, E. (1950). *Dementia Praecox or the Group of Schizophrenics.* New York: International University Press.

Bockar, J. (1976). *Primer for the Nonmedical Psychotherapist.* New York: Spectrum Publications.

Buber, M. (1937). *Between Man and Man.* London: Paul Kegan.

Buber, M. (1947). "Elements of the Interhuman." *Psychiatry.* Vol. 20, pp. 106–107.

Camus, A. (1942). *The Stranger.* New York: Vintage Books.

Camus, A. (1955). *The Myth of Sisyphus.* New York: Alfred Knopf.

Camus, A. (1980). *Neither Victims Nor Executioners.* New York: Continuum.

151

Celani, D. (1976). "An Interpersonal Approach to Hysteria." *American Journal of Psychiatry.* Vol. 12, pp. 1414–1418.

Corlis, R. and Rabe, P. (1969). *Psychotherapy from the Center.* Scranton: International Testbook Company.

Dixon, S. (1979). *Working with People in Crisis.* St. Louis: C.V. Mosby.

Ellis, A. (1962). *Reason and Emotion in Psychotherapy.* New York: Lyle Stuart.

Fabry, J. (1968). *The Pursuit of Meaning.* New York: Harper and Row.

Farber, L. (1957). "What is Effective in the Therapeutic Process." *American Journal of Psychoanalysis.* Vol. 17, pp. 21–26.

Fidler, G. and Fidler, J. (1978). "Doing and Becoming: Purposeful Action and Self-Actualization." *American Journal of Occupational Therapy.* Vol. 32, pp. 305–310.

Frank, J. (1961). *Persuasion and Healing.* New York: Schoken Books.

Frankl, V. (1953). "Logos and Existence in Psychotherapy." *American Journal of Psychotherapy.* Vol. 7, pp. 8–15.

Frankl, V. (1958). "On Logotherapy and Existential Analysis." *American Journal of Psychoanalysis.* Vol. 18, pp. 28–37.

Frankl, V. (1959). *Man's Search for Meaning.* New York: Simon and Shuster.

Frankl, V. (1965). *The Doctor and the Soul.* New York: Random House.

Frankl, V. (1969). *The Will to Meaning.* New York: New American Library.

Frankl, V. (1975). *The Unconscious God.* New York: Simon and Shuster.

Freud, S. (1933). *The Interpretation of Dreams.* New York: MacMillan.

Friedman, M. (1964). *The Worlds of Existentialism.* Chicago: The University of Chicago Press.

Gedo, J. (1979). *Beyond Interpretation.* New York: International University Press.

Gibran, K. (1923). *The Prophet.* New York: Alfred Knopf.

Glick, I. and Kessler, D. (1974). *Marital and Family Therapy.* New York: Grune and Stratton.

Gray, M. (1978). *Neurosis.* New York: Van Nostrant Reinhold.

Gregory, I. and Smeltzer, D. (1977). *Psychiatry.* Boston: Little, Brown and Company.

Grotjahn, M. (1960). *Psychoanalysis and the Family Neurosis.* New York: W.W. Norton.

Haley, J. (1963). *Strategies of Psychotherapy.* New York: Grune and Stratton.

Hammer, M. (1967). "The Directed Day Dream Technique." *Psychotherapy: Theory, Research and Practice.* Vol. 4, pp. 173–181.

Hollis, F. (1972). *Casework, A Psychosocial Therapy.* New York: Random House.

Horney, K. (1945). *Our Inner Conflicts.* New York: W.W. Norton.

Horney, K. (1950). *Neurosis and Human Growth.* New York: W.W. Norton.

Irons, P. (1978). *Psychotropic Drugs and Nursing Intervention.* New York: McGraw Hill.

Jellinek, E. (1960). *The Disease Concept of Alcoholism.* Highland Park: Hillhouse Press.

Kierkegaard, S. (1954). *The Sickness unto Death.* New York: Doubleday-Anchor.

Kolb, L. (1977). Modern Clinical Psychiatry. Philadelphia: W.B. Saunders.

Krill, D. (1968). "A Framework for Determining Client Modifiability." *Social Casework.* Vol. 49, pp. 602–611.

Krill, D. (1969). "Existential Psychotherapy and the Problem of Anomie." *Social Work.* Vol. 14, pp. 33–49.

Kubie, L. (1936). *Practical Aspects of Psychoanalysis.* New York: W.W. Norton.

Lantz, J. (1977). "Family Therapy: Using a Transactional Approach." *Journal of Psychosocial Nursing.* Vol. 15, pp. 17–22.

Lantz, J. (1978A). *Family and Marital Therapy.* New York: Appleton-Century-Crofts.

Latnz, J. (1978B). "Cognitive Theory and Social Casework." *Social Work*. Vol. 23, pp. 361–366.

Lantz, J. (1978C). "Co-therapy Approach in Family Therapy." *Social Work*, Vol. 23, pp. 156–158.

Lant, J. (1979). "Extreme Itching Treated by a Family Systems Approach." *International Journal of Family Therapy*. Vol. 1, pp. 244–253.

Lantz, J. (1980). "Adlerian Concepts: A Caseworker's Review." *Clinical Social Work Journal*. Vol. 8, pp. 188–197.

Lantz, J. (1981). "Depression and Social Interest Tasks." *Journal of Individual Psychology*. Vol. 37, pp. 113–116.

Lantz, J. (1982A). "Dereflection in Family Therapy with Schizophrenic Clients." *International Forum for Logotherapy*. Vol. 5, pp. 119–122.

Lantz, J. (1982B). "Meaning in Family Therapy." *International Forum for Logotherapy*. Vol. 5, pp. 44–46.

Lantz, J. (1982C). "Adlerian Community Treatment with Schizophrenic Clients." *Psychosocial Nursing*. Vol. 20, pp. 25–30.

Lantz, J. (1984A). "Responsibility and Meaning in Treatment of Schizophrenics." *International Forum for Logotherapy*. Vol. 7, pp. 26–28.

Lantz, J. (1984B). "The Noetic Curative Factor in Group Therapy." *International Forum for Logotherapy*. Vol. 7, pp. 121–123.

Lantz, J. (1984C). "Growth Stages in Logotherapy." *International Forum for Logotherapy*. Vol. 7, pp. 118–120.

Lantz, J. (1985A). "Dereflection and the Reduction of Depression in Relatives of Schizophrenic Clients." *International Forum for Logotherapy*. Vol. 8, pp. 49–53.

Lantz, J. (1985B). "Never Trust a Family Therapist Under Forty." *Voices*. Vol. 21, pp. 18–19.

Lantz, J. (1985C). "Logotherapy and the Person of the Therapist, An Open Systems Approach." *International Forum for Logotherapy*. Vol. 8, pp. 96–99.

Lantz, J. (1986A). "Treatment Motivation and Social Work Practice." (Unpublished paper).

Lantz, J. (1986B). "Integrating Task Centered and Reflective Techniques in Family Treatment." *Child Welfare*. Vol. 56, pp. 94–103.

Lantz, J. (1986C). "Family Logotherapy." *Contemporary Family Therapy*. Vol. 9, pp. 124–135.

Lantz, J. and Boer, A. (1974). "Adolescent Group Membership Selection." *Clinical Social Work Journal*. Vol. 2, pp. 172–181.

Lantz, J., Early, P. and Pillow, W. (1980). "Family Aspects of Trichotillomania." *Journal of Psychiatric Nursing*. Vol. 18, pp. 23–27.

Lantz, J. and Lenahan, B. (1976). "Referral-Fatigue Therapy." *Social Work*. Vol. 21, pp. 239–241.

Lantz, J. and Treece, N. (1982). "Identity Operations and Family Treatment." *Psychosocial Nursing*. Vol. 20, pp. 20–23.

Lantz, J. and Thorward, S. (1985). "Inpatient Family Therapy Approaches." *The Psychiatric Hospital*. Vol. 16, pp. 85–89.

Lieb, J. and Slaby, A. (1975). *Integrated Psychiatric Treatment*. New York: Harper and Row.

Lukas, E. (1981). "New Ways for Dereflection." *The International Forum for Logotherapy*. Vol. 4, pp. 13–28.

Mahler, M. (1958). "Autism and Symbiosis—Two Extreme Disturbances of Identity." *International Journal of Psychoanalysis.* Vol. 39, pp. 77–83.

Masterson, J. (1976). *Psychotherapy of the Borderline Adult: A Developmental Approach.* New York: Brunner-Mazel.

Mendelson, J. (1966). *Alcoholism.* Boston: Little, Brown and Company.

Mesaph, H. (1977). "Itching and Other Dematoses." In Wittkower, E. and Warnes, H. (Eds.). *Psychosomatic Medicine.* New York: Harper and Row.

Minuchin, S. (1974). *Families and Family Therapy.* Cambridge: Harvard University Press.

Mosak, H. (1977). *On Purpose.* Chicago: Alfred Adler Institute.

Mosak, H. (1979). "Adlerian Psychotherapy." In Corsini (Ed.). *Current Psychotherapies.* Itasca: F.E. Peacock Publishers.

Mullan, H. and Sangiuliano, I. (1964). *The Therapist's Contribution to the Treatment Process.* Springfield: Charles C Thomas, Publisher.

Munroe, R. (1955). *Schools of Psychoanalytic Thought.* New York: Dryden Press.

O'Connel, W. (1961). "Ward Psychotherapy with Schizophrenics Through Concerted Encouragement." *Journal of Individual Psychotherapy.* Vol. 17, pp. 193–204.

O'Connel, W. (1962). "Identification and Curability of the Mental Hospital Patient." *Journal of Individual Psychology.* Vol. 18, pp. 68–76.

Osipow, S., Walsh, B. and Tosi, D. (1980). *A Survey of Counseling Methods.* Homewood: Dorsey Press.

Perlman, H. (1979). *Relationship.* Chicago: University of Chicago Press.

Quaranta, J. (1971). "Conceptual Framework for Career Development Programming, in Wigtil, J. and McCormic, R. (Eds.). *Guidance for Planning and Evaluative Career Development.* Columbus: The Ohio Department of Education.

Rabkin, R. (1977). *Strategic Psychology.* New York: New American Library.

Rado, S. (1958A). "From the Meta-Psychological Ego of the Biocultural Action Self," *Journal of Psychology.* Vol. 46, pp. 279–290.

Rado, S. (1958B). "Psychotherapy: A Problem of Controlled Intercommunication," in Hoch, P. (Ed.), *Psychopathology of Communication.* New York: Grune and Stratton.

Rado, S. (1965). "Relationship of Short-Term Psychotherapy to Developmental Stages of Maturation and Stages of Treatment Behavior," in Wolberg, L. (Ed.), *Short-Term Psychotherapy.* New York: Grune and Stratton.

Raymond, J., Slaby, A. and Lieb, J. (1975). *The Healing Alliance.* New York: W.W. Norton.

Rogers, C. (1961). *On Becoming a Person.* Boston: Houghton Mifflin.

Rowe, C. (1980). *An Outline of Psychiatry.* Debuque: W.M. Brown Company.

Sartre, J.P. (1946). "American Novelists in French Eyes." *Atlantic Monthly.* Vol. 178, pp. 114–118.

Satir, V. (1967). *Conjoint Family Therapy.* Palo Alto: Science and Behavior Books.

Schwartz, E. (1960). "Recent Observations on Group Psychotherapy with Adolescent Delinquent Boys in Residential Treatment." *International Journal of Group Psychotherapy.* Vol. 10, pp. 195–212.

Sherman, M. (1982). "Psychoanalysis and Emotion." *Voices.* Vol. 18, pp. 40–42.

Shulman, B. (1962). "The Meaning of People to the Schizophrenic and the Manic-Depressive." *Journal of Individual Psychotherapy.* Vol. 18, pp. 151–156.

Slavson, S. (1951). "Current Trends in Group Psychotherapy." *International Journal of Group Psychotherapy.* Vol. 1, pp. 7–15.

Snyder, S. (1980). *Biological Aspects of Mental Disorders.* New York: Oxford University Press.

Spiegelberg, H. (1972). *Phenomenology in Psychology and Psychiatry.* Evanston: Northwestern University Press.

Starr, A. (1977). Psychodrama: *Rehearsal for Living.* Chicago: Nelson-Hall.

Stewart, R. (1981). "Building an Alliance Between the Families of Patients and the Hospital: Model and Process." *Journal of the National Association of Private Psychiatric Hospitals.* Vol. 12, pp. 63–69.

Strupp, H. (1959). "Towards an Analysis of the Therapist's Contribution to the Treatment Process." *Psychiatry.* Vol. 22, pp. 349–362.

Sullivan, H. (1946). *The Language of Schizophrenia.* New York: W.W. Norton.

Torrey, E. (1972). *The Mind Game: Witchdoctors and Psychiatrists.* New York: Emerson Hall.

Torrey, E. (1983). *Surviving Schizophrenia.* New York: Harper and Row.

Tosi, D. (1977). *Youth Towards Personal Growth: A Rational Emotive Approach.* Columbus: Charles E. Merrill.

Turner, F. (1978). *Psychosocial Therapy.* New York: The Free Press.

Wheelis, A. (1958). *The Quest for Identity.* New York: W.W. Norton.

Whitaker, C. and Malone, T. (1953). *The Roots of Psychotherapy.* New York: Brunner-Mazel.

White, R. (1971). "The Urge Toward Competence." *American Journal of Occupational Therapy.* Vol. 25, pp. 271–274.

Wolfe, A. and Schwartz, E. (1971). "Psychoanalysis in Groups." In Kaplan, H. and Sadock, B. (Eds.). *Comprehensive Group Psychotherapy.* Baltimore: Williams and Wilkins.

Wolpe, J. (1958). *Psychotherapy by Reciprocal Inhibition.* Stanford: Stanford University Press.

Yalom, I. (1970). *Theory and Practice of Group Psychotherapy.* New York: Basic Books.

Yalom, I. (1980). *Existential Psychotherapy.* New York: Basic Books.

Yalom, I. (1981). *Inpatient Group Psychotherapy.* New York: Basic Books.

Zuk, G. (1967). "Triadic-Based Family Therapy." *International Journal of Psychiatry.* Vol. 8, pp. 539–548.

Zuk, G. (1972). *Family Therapy: A Triadic Based Approach.* New York: Behavioral Publications.

# INDEX